Praise for **The Garage Girl's Guide**

*Courtney Hansen's automotive pedigree runs deep. Her father is a legend in SCCA racing and though she didn't go the racing route herself, Courtney has parlayed her knowledge, experience and passion into a career in automotive television and in the garage. Courtney's book is fun and personal, but based on fact and substance. It meets an important need!*

MARIO ANDRETTI

*Always the professional on film, through written word or during a simple, friendly conversation, Courtney Hansen leads you on a journey both entertaining and educational. With her All-American "Girl-Next-Door" looks and enthusiasm, Courtney truly knows how to brighten your day.*

CHIP FOOSE
AUTOMOTIVE DESIGNER/TV PERSONALITY,
THREE-TIME RIDLER AWARD WINNER

*When Courtney Hansen first splashed on the scene on* Overhaulin' *most people figured she was just some actress hired to host the show. Well, fortunately, that actress knows what she's talking about because she has been around custom cars, garages, and racing all her life. She's not a pretender, she knows how it really is, and that is refreshing. As a female, she brings a unique insight and perspective to cars and the automotive world. And the best part is she's sharing that knowledge and experience with others, as a girl who is "just one of the guys." Courtney Hansen is the real deal.*

STACEY DAVID
DESIGNER/BUILDER/TV HOST

*This guide is a must read for everyone from the car connoisseur to the auto-rookie. Courtney's perspective is valuable and is based on a lifetime of auto experience from the race track to the repair shop to the dealership to the TV show studio.*

THOMAS L. DUPONT
PUBLISHER, *THE DUPONT REGISTRY* AND
*CELEBRITY CAR MAGAZINE*

Me and Mom with Paul Newman.

*During the years that I was in auto races with Jerry Hansen, Courtney was always there—immersed in the track and garage action. She is a true car enthusiast.*

PAUL NEWMAN

*I've raced at the once Hansen-owned BIR Raceway and did many auto show appearances with Courtney where we talked cars, racing, and horsepower. She knows her stuff and has hardcore enthusiasm for all things automotive! Courtney's book is written with personality and contains her own stories, photos, and the basic ammunition needed to successfully purchase, care for, trick out, and sell a car. It's a guide for the masses!*

TONY SCHUMACHER
TOP FUEL DRIVER, U.S. ARMY,
THREE-TIME WORLD CHAMPION

*"I have had the pleasure of working with Courtney on* Overhaulin' *and now as part of the* Powerblock *team. Her enthusiasm for wanting to get as deep and dirty as possible in her constant drive for more information about the automotive world is an untouchable trait; one that many strive for yet is difficult to attain. Courtney has dedicated her life to sharing that knowledge and has expressed a wonderful quality by wanting to teach all that she knows and impart the skills she has learned onto others. I am blessed to have her as a co-worker and, of course, as a friend.*

JESSI COMBS
HOST OF XTREME 4X4,
FEMALE FABRICATOR AND MECHANIC

*Courtney Hansen's new book is loaded with car tips, facts and opinions from America's original "Garage Girl." This woman has high test running through her veins! If you want more out of the buying, driving and entire car experience, you need to read Courtney's book.*

JOE ST. LAWRENCE
EXECUTIVE PRODUCER, HORSEPOWER TV, TRUCKS!

# The
# GARAGE GIRL'S GUIDE

## TO EVERYTHING YOU NEED TO KNOW
## ABOUT YOUR CAR

# The GARAGE GIRL'S GUIDE

## TO EVERYTHING YOU NEED TO KNOW ABOUT YOUR CAR

### COURTNEY HANSEN

Foreword by JERRY HANSEN
Former SCCA Champion

CUMBERLAND HOUSE
NASHVILLE, TENNESSEE

THE GARAGE GIRL'S GUIDE TO EVERYTHING YOU
NEED TO KNOW ABOUT YOUR CAR
PUBLISHED BY CUMBERLAND HOUSE PUBLISHING
431 Harding Industrial Drive
Nashville, Tennessee 37211

Cover design: Gore Studio, Inc. (www.gorestudio.com)
Book design: Mary Sanford
Photography and cover image: Jason Christopher (www.jasonchristopher.com)
and Courtney Hansen
Diagrams: Dale Glasgow of Glasgow Media (dale@glasgowmedia.com)
Additional photography: Greg Meyer

**Library of Congress Cataloging-in-Publication Data**
Hansen, Courtney, 1976–
  The Garage girl's guide to everything you need to know about your car /
Courtney Hansen.
      p. cm.
  Includes bibliographical references and index.
  ISBN-13: 978-1-58182-519-0 (pbk. : alk. paper)
  ISBN-10: 1-58182-519-6 (pbk. : alk. paper)
  1. Automobiles—Maintenance and repair—Popular works.  I. Title.

TL152.H33 2006
629.28'72—dc22

                                                    2006027993

Printed in the United States of America
1 2 3 4 5 6 7—13 12 11 10 09 08 07

*I dedicate this book to God—I'm so thankful for His blessings in my life—*
*and to my amazing family and treasured friends,*
*who have always demonstrated unconditional love and support.*

# Contents

# Foreword

My daughter Courtney has been a part of the automotive world since the day she was born. She traveled with her mother, brother, sister, and me to racetracks and ice-races across the country in the family motor home. She spent every summer at Brainerd International Raceway, then co-owned by our family, hanging out in the pits, the garages, and the thick of the culture. Courtney met and watched many of the world's elite racecar drivers like Mario Andretti, Jackie Stewart, and Paul Newman and witnessed monumental events like Shirley Muldowney winning the national championship in drag racing at BIR. Courtney always loved taking in the action, asking the mechanics and drivers questions and learning more about this sport and industry. She worked on vehicles and, of course, she drove them!

While other girls were playing with Barbie dolls and having tea parties, Courtney was taking friends for rides in official pace-cars and touring the racetrack on mopeds. Courtney has been operating boats, cars, snowmobiles, motorcycles, four-wheelers, Jet Skis, motor homes, golf carts, go-karts, and anything else with an engine since she was old enough to grab hold of the wheel. Her mother and I believed in instilling confidence in our children by allowing them this privilege, and as a result Courtney became a

Working on Lance
Armstrong's GTO.

true enthusiast. She also became a very skilled driver. And
although she didn't choose to go the racing route because she had
other objectives in mind, if she had, I know she would have been
a winner.

Many years ago, Sam Moses from *Sports Illustrated* came to
Minneapolis to do a story on my SCCA racing career. During the
interview, he asked me to explain the difference between winning
and taking second place—my personal opinion on what separates
the winner from the rest. I pondered his question for a moment
before responding that winning isn't really about the mechanics of
driving or the pit crew; it isn't even about the car. There are and
have been lots of talented drivers in the sport with strong cars and
great crews. But there are very few consistently dominant winners.
Those who win consistently have an innate inner strength and

need that is very unusual. Every personal and business decision and sacrifice is made with a goal in mind. They don't just *want* to win; they *have* to win! Winners put themselves in the best position to win before the race even begins. Then, when the race is on, they have a willful determination few can match. When their car is not handling right, or they find themselves behind, they fight even harder. They dig deeper within themselves for strength, even when they feel they are already doing their best. Winners do what they have to in order to make it happen.

Courtney isn't a racecar driver. But she was born with the mentality and attitude of a winner. She has always been determined to accomplish her goals in every facet of her life. She never

lost sight of her career dreams and is accomplishing them. She has never allowed short-term defeat or rejection to dilute her long-term agenda or affect her belief in herself. Courtney's character has remained consistent since childhood. She sees the desired destination, maps out the best route, and then drives toward her goal with an unwavering determination. She is admired not only by me but by all of her family and friends for achieving one goal after another, yet allowing us to enjoy her journey with her. And, best of all, she has never compromised her morals or values along the way.

About five years ago Courtney decided to leave her corporate job and home in Florida to head to Los Angeles, a city she had never before visited, to pursue a full-time career in television. I have always supported her completely. However, my fatherly instinct urged me to properly warn and protect my daughter about this huge decision to move west on her own to pursue one of the most difficult occupations. As she was ready to leave for L.A. with bags packed and without money, a car, friends, family, or familiarity with the city, I said, "You know, Courtney, there are thousands of people who go to Hollywood every day in hopes of making it there. Very few actually do." And she looked at me and said, "Dad, I have your winning mentality. There is only one outcome for me." She was right. In spite of rejections, closed doors, and discouragement along the way, she worked hard and made it. Courtney is a winner.

I never missed an episode of *Overhaulin'*, I proudly watch Courtney every weekend as the host of Spike TV's automotive *Powerblock* and Fox Sports Net's *Destination Wild*, and I know there will be many more projects to come. It's not only amazing to see that Courtney has attained her goals and is doing what she

Below, Dad gives me an early driving lesson in our motor home, and to the right is Dad with me and my sister at Brainerd.

truly loves, but it's fun that these shows and this book involve her immense passion for the automotive world. The fact that children relate to her, men respect her, and women are inspired by what she's doing doesn't at all surprise me. Her mom and I couldn't be more proud.

Courtney's book is written from the heart and is based on her personal experiences, stories, and knowledge. I hope you enjoy it.

JERRY HANSEN

27-TIME SPORTS CAR CLUB OF AMERICA NATIONAL CHAMPION,

THE WINNINGEST DRIVER IN THE HISTORY OF THE SCCA,

AND COURTNEY'S FATHER

# The
# GARAGE GIRL'S GUIDE
## TO EVERYTHING YOU NEED TO KNOW
## ABOUT YOUR CAR

Left: Accepting the Ford Fusion "Life in Drive" Award. Below: Hanging out on the *Powerblock* set.

*Above:* On the *Overhaulin'* set in Ian Ziering's Camaro before its transformation. *Right:* At a 3M-sponsored NASCAR race in Detroit.

# *Introduction*

I'm thrilled you are reading my book because it means you are excited about the vehicle you want to buy or are interested in learning more about cars and how to care for the ride you already own. It really makes me happy when people share my passion for the automotive world. I love cars—the way they look, the way they sound, the way they perform, and the way they handle! Cars are such detailed, beautiful machines. In my opinion, they are one of the most important things we will ever own. They do much more than get us where we need to go. The vehicles we drive are also extensions of who we are. Because they reflect our identity, I feel we should take great care to make sure they are the right fit for our lives and will serve us in the best possible way for years to come.

Cars have been a huge part of my life since the day I was born. Many of my fondest childhood memories involve traveling in the family motor home from racetrack to racetrack across the United States, listening to Kenny Rogers and Willie Nelson tunes and supporting my dad's SCCA racing career. As a young girl I knew I was riding around with one of the greatest drivers in the world. For us kids, that was pretty cool, but at times also kind of scary. I have countless memories of my dad quickly and aggressively maneuver-

As you can see, my childhood was filled with vehicles of all kinds!

ing through traffic at high speeds to get us to school or tennis lessons on time! Having spent such a large part of my life at our family's old racetrack, Brainerd International Raceway—watching the races with Mom and friends, playing in the dirt with my sister and brothers, hanging in the pits and garages, watching the mechanics at work, and admiring the cars and their engines—that I grew up feeling incredibly at home at the racetrack and in the garage.

Although I decided not to become a racecar driver myself, I have always been a gearhead and have naturally gravitated toward everything automotive. While in high school I was fortunate enough to be hired by a local Dodge dealership to do more than twenty of their regional TV commercials. I had so much fun with the commercials, and this was when I realized I wanted to work in front of the camera for a living. Years later, I made the move to L.A. by myself to try to make it as a TV host, hoping that my love for cars would somehow be incorporated into my career, as it had in the past. During those first few years I worked in three restaurants simultaneously to make enough money to continually update my demo reel, portfolio, and headshots and be able to afford hosting classes. Then, after those couple of years of strug-

gling, I was thrilled when I was given the opportunity to work as a spokesperson for Rolls-Royce Motorcar, Ltd. It helped alleviate my hardcore restaurant schedule and gave me the chance to work with cars again. Then, about three years into life in L.A., my agent called to tell me that TLC was holding auditions for a car makeover show called *Overhaulin'*. Of course I was not only eager to be hands-on with cars again, but the show would give me the opportunity to work with many great mechanics and builders, and Chip Foose, a legendary automotive designer and fabricator. I went online and studied everything I could about auto mechanics as a quick refresher course in order to have a successful audition. The audition went well, and something inside of me made me feel very hopeful about booking the job. I was beyond grateful when I found out that I did.

After learning the news, I decided that I wanted to be more than just another host, strictly narrating or pretending to know about and be interested in the topic at hand. Cars are in my blood and have always been a major part of my life. So I wanted to share my knowledge and experience, while of course continuing to learn more. I chose to step beyond regular hosting duties by joining the build teams in the deconstruction and rebuilding of the *Overhaulin'* vehicles and, consequently, I believe I earned some respect from the men in the garage and the viewers at home.

*Overhaulin'* led to two other one-off TLC television specials, *Rides: Biggest Spenders* and *Million Dollar Motors*. Then in 2005, I started a new job hosting Spike TV's *Powerblock,* a weekend two-hour block of automotive shows, comprised of *Horsepower TV, MuscleCar, Xtreme 4x4,* and *Trucks!* I took over for IRL racer Danica Patrick, the former host, and I couldn't be happier in this position.

Although I knew my fair share about cars and engines before beginning work on *Overhaulin'*, I wanted to absorb as much information as I could and further hone my knowledge. So I made a trip to the bookstore and purchased every book I could find that dealt with car fabrication and auto mechanics. I sat on the beach outside my apartment in Marina del Rey, California, and read and highlighted the books every day for months. Two things happened as a result of this. First, I learned a whole lot more about the craft, which has made me much more confident in this male-dominated industry. And secondly, I quickly discovered that there was a need for a book that appealed to women and those who know very little about cars, that wasn't purely technical, that was written from the standpoint of maintaining cars and trucks on a daily basis. I saw this need and wanted to meet it.

About a year and a half ago I joined with Tekno Books and Cumberland House Publishing and began writing this book with a vision in mind. I set out to make the content informative, yet fun and personal. I wanted to incorporate stories and photos from my own experiences with the vehicles I drive and my time spent on racetracks, automotive TV sets, and in garages. I wanted to answer every question I've had along the way and cover the fundamentals that I believe are important for every car owner to know. I wanted the book to include everything from the process of purchasing a car or truck to how to properly maintain it, to how to handle emergency situations, to how to trick it out . . . and I wanted to address the question I'm asked most frequently, which is how to avoid getting ripped off by mechanics!

In the past few years in the automotive world some people began calling me the "Garage Girl." I couldn't have asked for a cooler nickname. The name, which may now be obvious, is where

Working with Foose on Lance Armstrong's '70 GTO.

the book title originated. But this book is my guide for anyone who wants to learn more about cars, as opposed to being strictly a guide for girls. Although I saw a need for a book written by a woman that speaks to women, I believe there are teens and men who will benefit from the material too.

*The Garage Girl's Guide* took me almost two years to write, and although it was tough at times and there were many sleepless nights, it has been an amazing, gratifying process. My heart is definitely in it!

Fixing a quarter panel on *Overhaulin'* with my friend Matt Harris.

It's obviously my hope that you will learn something in order to be better informed about how to properly care for your ride, and be more prepared, and therefore much safer in the event of emergencies. (I promise you that will happen!) But beyond that, I

Polishing a Hummer on the *Powerblock* set.

hope that, whether you're shopping for a ride or already own one, this book will help you understand the benefits of proper auto maintenance and ultimately make you more excited about and connected with your car or truck than ever before.

Many people take their daily drivers for granted. They never learn about their vehicles, and so cars just become a mode of transportation, rather than something to truly appreciate and enjoy. We spend countless hours on our hobbies, whether collecting coins, playing poker or sewing quilts. If we also make knowing our vehicles a great hobby, imagine how awesome it will be when the countless hours we spend driving and caring for our vehicles are transformed into one of our favorite activities. Thank you for allowing me the opportunity to share my passion with you. While reading this book it's my hope that you will develop a greater passion for your own ride. Have fun!

# FINDING YOUR RIDE

The process of purchasing or leasing a ride is exciting! It's a time to explore what auto styles and amenities appeal to you, test drive cool vehicles, ponder how your lifestyle and needs affect what you want to drive, and eventually take home your new prized possession, which will hopefully be the ideal extension of you. Unlike many other possessions, this one won't sit on a shelf somewhere collecting dust. It will be with you daily, in good times and bad, taking you where you need to go and exemplifying your personality along the way. In many ways your ride will be like your new best friend. You'll need to give it love and care and in return you will truly appreciate it, trust it, and enjoy its company. The road ahead may not always be smooth. But it's my hope that you will purchase a car or truck that makes you feel at home when you're on the road, that you'll learn the fundamentals of auto maintenance so that you can properly care for your vehicle, and that, ultimately, you will connect with your ride the way that I connect with mine.

Shopping for a new vehicle is a lot of fun. But in order to make a successful purchase, the process should be done thoroughly and carefully. A car or truck is obviously a huge purchase, and there are a multitude of choices out there for you. You want to be sure you aren't making a hasty or purely emotional decision. And before taking on this tremendous financial responsibility, you want to be certain the vehicle you choose is the ideal fit for your life. I'm going to share with you my ideas for meeting your perfect match. Are you up for the hunt? This will be fun!

Before buying or leasing a vehicle, you have to first make sure you know what you like. The ones we like aren't always unattainable. If you see cars or car features that appeal to you when you're out around town, inquire about them. Each time I've done this the owners have been proud of their rides and happy to share their thoughts. Next you want to do research about the ride. There are many resources that will help educate you on the specific make and model you're considering. Automotive publications, trade magazines, the Internet, newspapers, and of course your family and peers are all excellent sources of information. I love reading automotive magazines because they compare vehicles and give thorough reviews on most popular makes and models of different price ranges. The Internet is also a very valuable tool for locating information quickly and cheaply.

When doing your homework, here are some of the questions I urge you to ask yourself and evaluate: How does the vehicle perform? How does it hold up after wear? What are its safety and reliability statistics? Is it comfortable for enduring long trips or many hours in traffic? Is manual or electronic transmission the better choice? Is it a 4-cylinder, V6, or V8 engine, and what's the most appropriate option? Is power or economy more important? Can I afford to fill a big tank? Have I fully researched and considered hybrid vehicles, and does this car come in a hybrid version? Is the vehicle dog friendly? Is it child friendly? Ultimately you want to ask yourself, Is this really the ride that's best for me and my needs, and is it safe and affordable?

1. **Passenger Seating—How many passengers are normally in your vehicle?** If you typically carpool groups of children, a two-seater convertible probably isn't the right choice. That may be obvious. However, you should also consider the flip side. If you rarely have more than two passengers in your ride, is it worth suffering the hefty gas bills in order to drive an SUV? Also, do you have dogs or do a lot of road-tripping or camping with groups of people? Do you carry lumber or other machinery or products for your job that would take space in the car? One of my friends in L.A. is a wardrobe stylist. She loves the body style of the Mercedes CLK convertible and purchased one. However, because her line of work entails transporting racks of clothing from stores to film sets daily, she quickly realized that the small convertible wasn't the right vehicle for her. She recently exchanged her car for a roomy SUV.

2. **Storage Space and Hauling Power—Do you need a significant amount of trunk space?** If you haul a lot of camping gear or are responsible for babysitting and feeding groups of kids, a big trunk will come in handy. If you typically transport things like surfboards, bikes, wheelchairs or musical equipment, you may want to think about an SUV or truck. Also, are you planning to tow things? Does your vehicle adapt well to a hitch? Does it have the size and towing power to pull a mobile home, boat, or horse trailer?

3. **Driving Terrain—Do you need an all-wheel drive vehicle?** If you go off-roading regularly or live in the mountains or in

snow country where the plowing is erratic and roads are often icy, you'll benefit from all-wheel drive vehicle. However, all-wheel drive will increase the sticker price and mean slightly higher maintenance and fuel costs. At one time, I drove a Land Rover in Florida. It was a great SUV, and I had a lot of fun driving it, but the 4-wheel drive definitely wasn't a necessity on those flat Florida roads. For taking trips to the mountains outside of L.A., or if I moved back to Northern Minnesota, it would be the ideal ride.

4. **Maintenance & Fuel costs—How much driving do you do? What is the vehicle's average gas mileage?** With fuel prices rising steadily, gas mileage and cost of fuel are important considerations. Hybrid and electric vehicles cut down on gas bills and are eco-friendly. Auto manufacturers are making both hybrid and electric cars and hybrid SUVs, and the styling continues to improve considerably. You should look at the gas mileage for both city and highway driving and consider what you do more frequently. A hybrid could cut your gas bills in half.

5. **Reliability and the cost and availability of replacement parts—you need to prioritize how much these things matter to you.** A friend of mine swears by Volvos for reliability but admits that replacement parts can be a little pricy. For her, fewer trips to the repair shop makes up for the premium prices of parts. But that's something you should keep in mind while shopping. Generally, domestic car parts will be cheaper than those for imports, and the more expensive your car was, the more you are probably going to pay for replacement parts. Also, if you drive a common car or truck, parts for it will be more reasonable and readily available. Be aware that

Driving my Foosed-out '04 T-bird.

the amount of money you'll spend on your vehicle during its lifetime by no means ends with the initial purchase price.

6.  **What is the vehicle's blue book value?** It's important to know the established standard pricing of the make and model you are considering and the cost of each of the options/features you will choose. Having this information will allow you to plan your budget and know instantly if you are being snowed by a salesperson, particularly if the vehicle is a used model. Blue Book values for new cars usually show up the following year. Knowing the numbers and being informed will save you time and money. The figures are available in volumes you can purchase at most bookstores, auto stores, and online.

7.  **Does this vehicle hold its value well?** Research the resale value of the car or truck you are thinking of purchasing and

see how it and its current engine are predicted to perform in the long run. Again, these figures are easy to locate on the Internet. Some vehicles, such as restored classics, luxury cars, and limited edition models hold their value extremely well.

Isn't she beautiful? I love how the porthole windows and body style are reminiscent of '56 and '57 T-Birds.

I asked myself all of those questions and spent months pondering and discussing the various choices before making a decision. Before buying my 2004 Thunderbird two years ago, I had considered purchasing a '57 T-Bird or a '65 Mustang to use as my daily driver. When I talked with my dad about this, he urged me to rethink that idea. Both are great cars, but they are also both old, less reliable, and without warranties. With the amount of driving I do, frequently to faraway destinations and during late night hours, neither of those cars was a wise choice.

On the other hand, my two-seater T-Bird is not the kind of car that's practical for children or big dogs, and it isn't suited for driving on rough or mountainous terrain. It's also not the best choice for carrying surfboards or pulling a boat. So I had to evaluate whether or not these factors were important to me at this time in my life and weigh it all into the equation. I also considered the advantages of both automatic and manual transmissions. A manual transmission is more fun to drive but might have made driving in the city and through daily L.A. traffic a little tough. I opted for the automatic version. The engine is a high-performance, 3.9-liter V8 that is powerful and produces a killer rumbling sound. Although gas bills are a little steep, I'm willing to forgo that minor drawback because I love the car and feel it's perfect for my lifestyle.

At this point in my life, I don't have kids, so a two-seater is fine. I also don't have to carry big machinery or sporting equipment for my job. If I intend to pull a boat or travel with the dogs for a weekend, I'll rent an SUV or go in a friend's truck. The positive factors far outweigh the one con of higher gas bills. After pondering all of these questions I realized that, based on my needs, the 2004 T-Bird was the ideal vehicle choice for me.

### Does my oil need to be of a thinner viscosity for the winter months?

The answer is . . . it depends. If you drive an SUV, full-size truck, or one with more than eight-cylinders, experts agree the answer is no. Use oil that is formulated for larger engine vehicles. It will say "Truck/SUV" on the label. If you live in a geographic region where temperatures rarely dip below 20° fahrenheit, you can use the same oil year-round. However, if you live in an area of the country where temperatures dip very low on a regular basis (more than two to three weeks a year), and you drive a vehicle with a smaller engine (four to six cylinders), and especially if you're in the habit of cranking your engine and demanding high performance, you should consider a lower weight oil of a thinner viscosity for winter driving. Regardless of the oil you use, be sure to always have your oil changed before the first winter freeze.

### How often do I need to replace my brakes? Does it make a difference if the car is front- or rear-wheel drive?

Brakes need to be replaced when they begin to indicate wear. Some driving conditions require significantly more braking than others, so some drivers may go through a pair of pads every ten thousand miles, while a NASCAR vehicle can burn a pair after every race. You should have your brakes checked at least every ten thousand miles for wear, and more frequently if you spend a lot of time in traffic or typically drive in mountainous terrain. If you have a front wheel drive vehicle, the front brakes are more important and will need to be replaced more often, and the same holds true for cars with rear-wheel drive.

### What is a "HEMI"? Why is the Chrysler/Dodge name associated with Hemi engines? Are they better?

Back in the Musclecar era, Dodge developed and branded the HEMI engine, which had hemispherical cylinder heads, making for a cleaner and more powerful burn and producing more horsepower per cubic inch. Even today, when most vehicles have hemispherical engines, we relate HEMI with Dodge.

Your needs are undoubtedly different from mine, but the same idea applies. Take the time to ask yourself those questions and weigh the various factors. Try to be wise with your purchase. Remember, this is just your daily driver. There's a whole lifetime ahead for you to add dream rides to your collection.

# NEW, USED, OR LEASED?

**N**ow that you've begun your search for the perfect vehicle, you have some decisions to make. Are you going to buy a new or used car? Will you lease your car or own it outright? Are you going to pay for it in full or finance it? This chapter will address all of these questions and hopefully give you a better idea of the route you want to take.

## *Buying New*

There are many benefits to buying a new vehicle. To begin with, there's that fantastic new car smell! It's so appealing, in fact, that most car washes now sell "New Car Smell" air fresheners. One of the best reasons to buy new is the new car warranty (which is, sadly, *not* available at the car wash). Although you may never have to use it, your warranty is worth its weight in gold for the times when you do need it. New car warranty periods are typically three years long or 36,000 miles, whichever comes first, and they will cover just about everything from bumper to bumper. Some manufacturers offer longer warranties, but keep in mind that they will usually add to the overall price of your vehicle.

### Extended Warranties

Another option when buying a new car or truck is to consider purchasing an extended warranty. Different types of warranties may be offered from dealer to dealer, but if you decide to get one you should always insist on the actual manufacturer's warranty. For instance, if purchasing a new Ford, you would get the Ford ESP warranty. Unlike some aftermarket warranties, the Ford ESP is accepted at any Ford dealership in the United States. All manufacturers have their own form of extended warranties. Though dealerships could sell the manufacturer warranties, some will opt to make more money selling less expensive warranties that are only accepted at their location, or they will require you to do extra paperwork in order to use them. Please be cautious of these tactics.

There are several types of extended warranties. They range from the basic powertrain warranty (engine and transmission only) to full bumper-to-bumper coverage. You also have the option to choose the years and mileage of coverage, from 5/50,000 to 7/100,000, or any combination of these. Do you think you will only drive 50,000 miles in seven years or will you hit 100,000 miles in less than six years? You'll want to estimate your annual mileage and tailor a plan to best suit your needs.

You can also buy an extended warranty at a slightly higher price after having driven the vehicle for a while. But consider the cost of the warranty. Will it be easier for you to add a little cost to your monthly payments rather than pay one lump sum later on? That's up to you to decide.

Another benefit to buying new is that with the warranty also comes a relationship with a dealership that knows your vehicle well and will service your ride, inform you of any recalls, possibly offer you deals, and take good care of you and your car during the years you own it.

Because you will have an ongoing relationship with the dealership, I believe it's a good idea to know the reputation of the dealership you're considering buying from and how committed they are to their customers. It will behoove you to do a little research about them at the same time you're researching various rides. Drop in and ask all of the important questions about warranties, insurance plans, service agreements, etc. Also inquire about any special offers they currently have available.

Many years ago in Florida, after shopping for months for a BMW 325i, a dealer introduced me to an amazing opportunity. I ended up purchasing a car they referred to as a "Brass Hat," or demo car. The BMW didn't have many miles on it (only four hundred) and was basically brand new. But because it had been used as a demo and was driven from one city to another, thousands of dollars were knocked off the sticker price. Needless to say, I walked away extremely happy. This type of deal may not happen every day, but there are many opportunities available if you look around and inquire. It's definitely worth the effort.

For women, another advantage to buying new vehicles is that auto manufacturers are now offering features that appeal specifically to us, such as spaces for ponytails in the head rests (haven't seen them yet, but I've heard about them), electronic pedal extenders for shorter drivers (usually women), spaces built for holding shopping and grocery bags, and removable/washable seat covers. Granted some men may find these features beneficial too. But they were created with women in mind, and it's great that the manufacturers are thinking of us.

### Dealer Tricks

Of course, there are also dealer tricks to watch out for when car shopping. Dealers generally don't make very much money on the sale of new cars. Their big bucks are made later in the sales of aftermarket parts and services. There are some dealer add-ons that increase their profit substantially while adding little or no value to the vehicle. Some examples of this are exterior/paint sealant, pre-loaded alarm systems, fuel maximizers, and underbody coating. If you are interested in these features, I recommend waiting and adding them later. It will save you money to purchase these items somewhere other than the dealership.

### Financing

You have the option to pay in full at the time you purchase your ride, or you can do what's called financing. Financing a car or truck will allow you to pay for the vehicle monthly rather than in one initial lump sum. Some people confuse this with leasing, but with financing you own the car, and the payments are just applied toward what you owe. The penalty for this is that you will have to pay monthly interest, and those figures can be steep depending on the deal you are able to get. If you'll be financing your ride, you should bring your proof of full-coverage insurance along with you. If you have less than stellar credit, also bring your pay stubs, other proof of income, your home phone bill, and ten references (all referred to as "stips"), as you will need these in order to finance your vehicle as well.

Before financing, the dealer will have to run your credit report. They cannot promise you an interest rate or monthly payment number without first running your scores. You may have to run it several times as you shop from dealership to dealership looking for the best deal. I was always told that running credit reports too many times hurts credit scores. This is a fallacy. You can actually have your credit run at several different dealerships without it adversely affecting your credit score because the major credit reporting agencies understand that buyers are shopping around. Unlike applying for credit cards with retail stores, which will hurt your scores, you can have five, ten, even twelve dealerships run your credit in about a two-week period, and it will only count as one inquiry on your credit report.

Also, it's not a good idea to buy a car just before purchasing or refinancing a home. This is a huge red flag for mortgage companies. It shows that you have too many monthly expenses to incur, and the lender will be skeptical about your ability to make your monthly mortgage payments.

Here's a tip the dealer will never tell you about. When shopping for your ride, go to the dealership armed with the best interest rate you can locate on your own. This bit of homework could save you thousands. Credit unions usually offer the best rates, so check with yours or think about joining one. Chances are that you know someone who is a member of a great credit union.

Take that rate to the dealer and ask them to beat it. If they are able to, they will. Dealers can have more than two hundred banks and lending institutions to choose from. Make them work to come to *your* terms, rather than the other way around.

If you ever feel uncomfortable in the process of car shopping and negotiating, get up and take a walk. The overwhelming thought of having to incur the down payment and monthly expenses can be understandably stressful. You'll think more clearly and do a better job negotiating if you get up and take a breather.

### Negotiating the Rate

When negotiating the monthly payment, remember to focus on the *actual price* of the car. Most dealerships use a system called a "four-square." In four different quadrants on a page are trade value, MSRP (or the price of the new car), down payment, and monthly payments, all later to be massaged and adjusted (usually to the dealer's advantage). During what is called the "first pencil," the salesman will usually throw out some high numbers in the monthly payment and down payment boxes, focusing on how much you are able to put down and what you will pay monthly. Then the salesman will return to the sales office (sometimes referred to as the "desk" or "tower"), before coming back to you with the worksheet now covered in marker. They usually want to keep you focused on payment, not the actual price of the vehicle. And with your down payment, trade value, and interest rate, even Dustin Hoffman's *Rain Man* couldn't calculate these complicated numbers!

While this is happening, you should remain focused on the quadrant that shows MSRP, or the price of the car. Insist on discussing the price of the car, and let *that* dictate the payments. If you do this correctly, the salesman will typically bring his manager or team leader over to you. This person is often referred to as the "closer." The closers are good. But I urge you to stick to your guns and stay focused on the price. If the closer does not follow along, ask to see the vehicle's invoice. It will give you time to regroup and will show that you are not going to be a "lay down," or someone who just agrees to the first set of numbers put in front of you. *Never* agree to the first set of numbers. I'm counting on you to be strong negotiators!

You should also be realistic. You aren't going to be able to purchase a brand new thirty thousand dollar car for three hundred bucks a month for 60 months with no money down (you will also have to factor in the taxes, license fees and interest). You *might* have the option of buying or leasing for a longer term, like 72 or even 84 months, but this is a bad idea, as it really only benefits the bank. A longer term may lower your monthly payments, but it will add considerable cost to the price of the vehicle over time. A longer term will also keep you from trading in the car, and you will be "upside down" for a longer period of time. I'll explain what that means in a moment.

## *Leasing*

The main advantage to leasing a vehicle is that less money is required for the down payment than if you purchased it. So you can get the same car for less money up front if you lease. Generally, a company will require just two months' payment upfront, just like an apartment where you pay the first and last month's rent. Leases also make sense when you don't want to spend a lot of time and energy maintaining the vehicle (although I encourage you to properly maintain any ride you drive.) After the lease expires, you can trade the current vehicle for the newer, updated version of the same make and model and get a brand new warranty with it. A newer car means a more reliable car. If you don't choose to swap the current model for a new one, you also have the option to purchase the vehicle when the lease term is up.

One minor disadvantage to leasing is that you are only permitted to go a certain number of miles per year during the term of the lease, and if at the time you turn the car in the mileage exceeds that set number, you pay additionally per mile. If you do a lot of driving, this can be a pretty significant number in the end. At the end of my term for a vehicle I leased, I had gone well beyond the fifteen thousand allotted miles per year and had a hefty sum to pay. Another drawback is that leasing costs about 20 percent more over three years than buying the vehicle directly because of the interest you're paying and the lack of any equity you would have built if you bought the car. And, obviously, you put all of this money into driving it, but own nothing in the end.

It's a misconception that leased vehicles offer greater tax advantages than owned cars. Business driving expenses are deductible whether the car is leased or owned. I drive my T-Bird so often for work that a major portion of it is deducted each year as a business expense, even though it is owned.

Leasing is certainly not for everyone, but here is something to think about: Did you know that a majority of the buyers at dealerships trade in a car or truck that they are still making payments on? Almost all of these buyers owe more than what the car is worth, which is called being "upside down." Have you ever heard the dealership tagline, "We'll pay off your trade no matter how much you owe"? Sure, they'll pay off your trade, but only *after* you pay them. That remaining balance you owe is added into the new deal, raising the price of the new vehicle.

Recently, a friend of mine who works at a dealership sold a car to a loyal return customer. The man was trading in his car after three and a half years of a five-year purchase agreement. As a trade, his car was worth $20,000. But he still owed $22,500 on it, making him "upside down." He owed $2,500 more than his car was worth as a trade in the sixty-month contract. The man had to add that $2,500 to the price of his new car. He has a continual payment to make, just like someone who leases would have (especially if he ends up trading this new car in before his contract is up). However, someone with a lease will never be upside down. If this man had gone with the lease option, he would not have owed a penny (assuming there was no damage to the vehicle and no extra mileage), *and* he would have moved right into his next new car, usually at a lower payment than buying and often with special lease-to-lease incentives.

If you want to trade your ride in every two to three years, always drive a new car, and own a vehicle that will continuously be under warranty (meaning virtually no repair costs), then leasing is the best option for you. If you are someone who plans to hold onto your ride for seven or more years, I suggest buying.

I made the decision to lease my first car in L.A., because I only intended to drive it for four years, and then purchase something to hold onto. Before leasing my ride, which was a VW Passat, I called dealerships from here to Las Vegas asking what their average monthly lease rate would be. I had been told the rates varied drastically from dealer to dealer. The prices in fact ranged from $650 a month in Beverly Hills to less than $300 per month in Ontario, California. That's a pretty unbelievable difference! It was obviously worth my while to drive further east to lease the car. With my decent credit score, I paid only $320 per month for a four-year lease on the Passat. It literally pays to spend time researching.

Also, before leasing the Passat, I had had my mind set on the more powerful V6 model. However, the 4-cylinder model was being offered for significantly less money monthly. The 4-cylinder *also* happened to be the last one the dealership had available, and because it had been driven from a dealer four hundred miles away they were offering a special deal on it. Needless to say, I ended up leasing the 4-cylinder and was grateful I did. The smaller engine also had much better fuel economy during a time when hefty gas bills wouldn't have been affordable for me. That little bit of diligence meant I saved a bundle on the lease, as well as on gas bills.

### *Buying Used*

Did you know that when you drive a new vehicle off the lot it typically loses about a third of its value the moment the tires hit the pavement? The most obvious advantage to buying a used car is that you can get killer deals.

Another benefit to purchasing a used vehicle is that the older classic cars and trucks have incredible vintage styling and appeal that has many buyers longing for those designs of decades passed. (For more on this, see the following section.)

Be aware, however, that shopping for used cars is a bit of a game. If you're good, the game can pay off with big rewards. If not, you could get burned and end up with some nasty and expensive surprises. Hopefully this chapter will help you become more comfortable with the buying process. If you don't have confidence in your knowledge and automotive savvy, I recommend bringing someone with experience along to help you. There's nothing wrong with that. Besides, it's someone to share the fun with!

Before buying any used vehicle, you should absolutely get a Carfax report based on the vehicle's VIN (Vehicle Identification Number) to review its history. Make sure the VIN numbers on the vehicle match what's on the report. On average, VIN numbers are found in at least four different locations on a vehicle, and I suggest locating them on your car or truck and making sure they all match perfectly. Common places for VINs are the dash, the doorjambs, inside the engine compartment, and on the inner fender wells. Because auto theft is such a growing problem, some manufacturers are now etching VIN numbers into the window glass. This is a deterrent because glass is so costly to replace. In addition to getting a Carfax report, ask the seller for the receipts for any work and maintenance that was done to the vehicle so you can be certain it actually was.

Don't be afraid to ask the seller or dealer a lot of questions, and make eye contact with them, being leery of any smooth talking or inaccurate information. It's important to understand as much as you can about the car and the owners who formerly drove it. You want to try to find out what they used it for, what climate it was driven in, what rust damage it contains, if it was involved in any accidents or floods or disasters, etc. I recently heard stories about some of the vehicles that were destroyed in Katrina and other hurricanes. Owners sometimes neglected to disclose information about water, rust, and engine damage. Please be very cautious of these types of scams. It's wonderful to donate money to the victims of disasters or organizations that help them. But I don't think you want to be driving a car that was a victim of a hurricane.

If you aren't a serious car person with an understanding of body work and mechanics, I highly recommend bringing along an expert who is to join you for the test drive and help you fully examine the body, interior, and engine. I've provided a detailed checklist to guide you through the process (see pages 41–43), but here are some of the most important points.

You'll want to examine the engine thoroughly for mechanical issues and inspect the vehicle's body for rust, damage, and shoddy repair work. Always bring a magnet and run it over the metal surface to check for patches of Bondo or body filler. (You'll want to put a thin cloth between the magnet and the body as a buffer to keep from scratching the car's paint job.) If your magnet doesn't stick to any part of the car's surface, that indicates that the vehicle

With my friend and favorite paint and body expert, Mitch Lanzini.

has had some poor bodywork done and Bondo has replaced or covered most of the metal in that area. Another method to test for Bondo repair is knocking on the car's body with your fist. The hollow sound that occurs when knocking on pure metal means the body is in good condition. You'll hear the distinct difference when you reach an area that's been filled with Bondo.

Bring along some cotton swabs (Q-tips) as well. The swabs can be used to wipe the inside of the vehicle's tailpipe. If a used car or truck has been burning oil and needs a ring job, the prospective seller will often clean out the tailpipe, but only as far in as they can reach. By taking a swipe inside the pipe, you can check farther in and look for signs of excessive oil residue. If the swab comes out with a glob of black oil on its tip, you know the engine is in need of repair. You should also check the ground beneath the engine and around the engine compartment for signs of fluid leakage.

Check the odometer and be cautious that it hasn't been tampered with. If you have your eye on a 1950 GMC truck, and the mileage gauge reads twenty thousand miles, I'd be cautious. (But don't worry; as we learned watching *Ferris Bueller's Day Off*, driving a car in reverse will not reduce the mileage!)

It's a good idea to ask around and do research in auto magazines, trade books, and online to be certain the seller or dealer is quoting a fair price for that make and model. Another valuable tool is the Kelly Blue Book. Their website is www.kbb.com. Their user-friendly program lets you look up used vehicles' values and pricing for retail, private party sales, or trade-ins.

Just like when purchasing new, it also pays to scour the market for deals and trade-in opportunities!

## Buying Vintage

The biggest advantage to buying vintage is the way the muscle cars and classics were designed—with power, performance, and impeccable styling in mind. The classics take us back in time, represent our beloved America, maintain their value, and, most importantly, make collectors and auto enthusiasts happy. The auto manufacturers have been trying to reinvent American Muscle and duplicate the classic styling of those older models. But to many people, nothing compares with the oldies. Personally, I love the muscle cars and classics. Some of my favorites are the old Mustangs, Corvettes, Thunderbirds, Camaros, Road Runners, Chargers, Chevelles, 'Cudas, and Challengers . . . and Firebirds and Ford, Chevy, and GMC trucks and. . . . You get my point! I don't think there's a classic I don't appreciate.

Keep in mind, however, that vintage rides aren't going to be as reliable as new cars, and you might have to add features like air conditioning, audio systems, and even power steering and brakes

My buddy paid three thousand dollars for a new paint job. That seems like a lot of money to me. What's the ballpark figure on a quality paint job? What makes a paint job good?

Three thousand dollars is actually a really low price, so low in fact that I'd be concerned it isn't going to be a quality job. When it comes to painting your vehicle, you definitely get what you pay for. A solid paint, color-sand, and buff job with a warranty should cost you roughly sixty-five hundred dollars and possibly much more. It depends largely on the size of the vehicle and the quality of the paint. Also, paint jobs are more expensive these days because the EPA has enforced stricter environmental laws on this industry. Their paint booths have to be more environmentally sound and meet strict ventilation standards.

Mitch Lanzini of Lanzini Body Works (where I take my T-Bird for body and paint repairs) explained to me

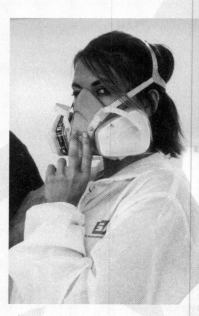

Painting requires the proper attire and safety gear.

that to sand and strip the previous paint job, lay down the coats of primer and paint, and do a thorough job of color sanding and buffing takes time and is a costly process. All layers of a chipped, flaky, or faded paint job must be stripped before applying new paint. Mitch says, "A new paint job requires a solid base to work on top of. An existing paint job can work as your primer if it's in great shape. But if it's in bad condition, it will need to be stripped to the bone, sanded, and prepared before laying any new primer or paint. This process is absolutely necessary for a quality job." For really high-end vehicles, the price gets even steeper. Chip Foose informed me that cars getting ready for an auto show or competition like the Ridler (Chip has won the Ridler Award three times) can spend months being painted and wet sanded. Also, for you red paint lovers, shades of red paint will generally cost an additional 3 percent for materials because of the difficulty in producing those shades. A paint job isn't just about a pretty color. Painting is a long, arduous, and layered process that requires time, patience and skill. It's truly an art form. A big part of the job actually happens after the layers of paint are laid down and have cured. The vehicle then has to be color sanded (or wet sanded) and buffed. This takes several days and accounts for about half of the labor costs. Color sanding removes the appearance of orange peel on the paint surface as well as any dust or dirt, making the vehicle look like a shining show car. Take care of your paint job, and it could last a lifetime.

I had the opportunity on a couple of *Overhaulin'* projects to paint body panels and engine parts on some of the cars. It amazed me how many layers of primer and paint are applied, even to parts in the engine compartment and inside or underneath the vehicle that we rarely see. The painter needs an adequate space or booth and of course, the proper paint suit and respirator mask to do the job right.

Sanding the roof of a car on *Overhaulin'*.

to make the driving experience more comfortable. Not to mention the fact that replacing parts and body panels can be difficult and expensive. I suggest calling around locally and also checking online and within specialty clubs to be sure most commonly replaced parts and body panels for the vehicle you're considering are readily available.

There are parts catalogs available at many auto parts stores and dealers, or they can be ordered from the specialty stores as well. During *Overhaulin'* builds we did a lot of work with parts stores like Original Parts Group in Southern California. OPG specializes in parts and panels for Chevy models. On both *Overhaulin'* and now the *Powerblock* shows, we do a lot of work with Year One. Year One is a huge supplier of replacement body panels for popular late model vehicles. When purchasing a used vehicle from a dealer or private party seller, be sure to find out if there is a parts catalog to accompany your ride.

A friend of mine is considering buying a '68 Firebird that he found at a local used car lot. He researched this model extensively online, went to the lot and test drove the car several times, and brought a mechanic with him to inspect the engine. He definitely did his homework. He's still not sure if it's within his budget, but if he buys the Firebird, he'll do so with confidence, prepared for the road ahead and knowing it's a worthy investment.

# TEST DRIVING AND INSPECTING

**I**t's now time to learn test-driving tips as well as how to conduct a thorough inspection of a vehicle's body, interior, and engine. I have complete faith in your ability to pull off a solid inspection at the dealership, but if you doubt yourself, go ahead and practice on your current vehicle or a friend's ride. You'll learn, and in the process you might also uncover little issues that need to be addressed with that other vehicle that will help increase its resale value later.

Following the checklist on pages 41–43 and doing the inspection in front of a seller will show them how serious you are. They will be less likely to take advantage of you, and it's also unlikely there will be any issues hidden from you.

This may sound like a no-brainer, but the time of day when you inspect the vehicle makes a difference. Be sure to schedule your inspection and test drive during daylight hours, preferably during strong light so that you can really see everything. Also, wet cars are deceiving because they make paint jobs look much better, so be wary of a seller who is showing you a ride that's wet.

Test-driving one of my all-time favorite classics, a '65 Mustang convertible.

I recommend arriving at the dealership early, especially if you're looking at used cars. If there's any last minute primping to cover obvious problems with the vehicle, you might catch the seller in the middle of it.

Take a test drive, and have fun. This is the greatest part! Test drive as many cars as possible so that you can compare them, and drive as long as the dealer will allow you to. I always ask the dealer to let me drive for a longer period of time because it isn't only about testing a ride's performance, but it's a time to listen to the car and get a feel for it as well. The sound of the engine will tell you a whole lot about the state of the vehicle's health. You want a smooth-running engine that ignites without problems, unless you are knowingly buying a classic junker to restore and you plan to make engine improvements.

During the test drive, turn the radio off, roll down the windows, and really listen to the engine while the car is moving. Problems that aren't apparent when a vehicle is idling will become clear once it's in motion. A good tip for detecting engine issues is to drive the car alongside a solid wall at about twenty miles per hour (the dealer's lot or a mall parking lot will work). Listen to the reflected sound. You'll hear things that you wouldn't normally notice in traffic. If the car purrs nicely, it's probably in pretty good shape under the hood. If it makes any strange noises it may be time to look at another model, or at least plan to knock the seller's purchase price down.

Make note of the exhaust sound and smell. Stinky emissions or a sputtering exhaust could signify engine troubles. Pay attention to the vehicle's handling, taking note of how the suspension reacts on bumps and turns. Make a couple of abrupt stops to see how the brakes feel. Accelerate a few times to see how the car responds. Whether it's a manual or electronic transmission, make sure the car is shifting gears fluidly. Transmissions are expensive to repair and extremely costly to replace. Make sure you like driving with a manual transmission. Check the blind spots. All cars have them, but be sure the visibility is okay for *you* and feels safe. For a brief moment, take your hands off the wheel to test for proper alignment. If the vehicle veers to one side, the alignment needs readjusting.

Test the cruise control, blinkers, speedometer, and all gauges to make sure they work properly. Roll the windows up and down to make sure they function well. When at a stoplight, test out the emergency brake. Make sure it releases correctly. If there is a convertible top, put it up and down a time or two while safely stopped. And, of course, make sure you feel comfortable in the driver's seat.

Once you are satisfied with the car's sound, smell, handling, and performance, you can move on to the visual inspection. This is going to take a while, so be sure to budget the time for it, and don't let the seller rush you.

You'll need:

- A flashlight and extra batteries.
- Rags or paper towels (heavy-duty paper towels are ideal)
- Hand cleaning wipes
- A notebook for keeping track of your discoveries
- A pen or pencil
- Cotton swabs (to check the exhaust for residue, as I mentioned earlier)
- A hand mirror for looking at areas that are hard to see directly, like under the car and in the nooks and crannies of the engine, wheel wells, and trunk.
- A small magnet (again, to test for Bondo or body filler on the body of the car)
- The checklist on the following pages.

## All Cars

| | |
|---|---|
| OK? | Walk around the outside of the vehicle. Are there any noticeable dings, scratches, rust, dents or other paint problems? Are there any inconsistencies in paint tone or texture? Run your hands along the vehicle's panels—touch will sometimes tell you more than your eyes can. Any detected problems can be used to negotiate the price down, if you are still determined to buy the car. |
| OK? | Inspect all seams—along the doors, trunk and hood, making sure they are straight, of consistent width, and the doors, trunk and hood open and close easily. If they aren't, it could mean shoddy workmanship, that the car suffered a wreck you haven't been informed about, or that something is out of balance or poorly installed and may later come back to haunt you. |
| OK? | Inspect the tires, making sure they're in good shape and have even tread wear patterns. If not, this can mean alignment problems, or possibly even a bent frame, which is a monster to repair. |
| OK? | Check underneath the car using a flshlight and hand mirror. Are there any signs of leakage of fluids under the car? |
| OK? | Check for any signs of rust or staining on the car's underside. Are there globs of hardened oil or rust? Rust found there probably means there is more disguised beneath the paint job. |
| OK? | Check for any suspicious scratches or other markings on the undercarriage o the car, which indicate the car may have bottomed out. Also look at the oil pan. Is it in good shape and without cracks? |
| OK? | Push on each corner of the car to see how the suspension reacts. The vehicle should bounce a couple of times and stop. If it doesn't, the suspension is too loose. Does the suspension seem firm enough? And does the vehicle sit level on its tires, before and after you bounced it? If it doesn't, there is a problem with the suspension. |
| OK? | Examine every part of the engine compartment. Is the engine clean and well cared for? Do any parts look shimmed up or rigged? Are there any abnormal stains that might signify fluid leaks? Is there staining around the radiator that would lead you to suspect that the car has overheated in the past? Are the belts and hoses in good shape, with no visible signs of cracking or tears? |

## All Cars (continued)

| | |
|---|---|
| OK? | Check all of the fluid levels. They should be topped up. Make sure to check the oil for quality, as well—is it clear and golden? Dirty oil is a sign that the car hasn't been well cared for, and this can be a predictor of engine trouble further down the road. |
| OK? | Open and close the doors. Are they smooth and well balanced? Do they seal tightly? How's the weather stripping? How does the paint look around the door edges? |
| OK? | Give the interior a sniff test. Do you smell mildew, dampness, or anything else that seems abnormal? Any foreign odors can mean possible problems, like condensation leaks from the air conditioner, leaky windows, or other issues. |
| OK? | You felt the drivers seat during the test drive. Now check the passenger seats as well. Are they comfy? |
| OK? | Adjust all the mirrors and check for blind spots. All vehicles have blind spots, but is the visibility ok for you? |
| OK? | Check the carpet for any stains, especially under the dash, at the top of the carpet. Are there any suspicious marks? If there are, it could mean condensation or heater core leaks. |
| OK? | Check out all of the switches and buttons. Do electric windows and locks operate smoothly, wiper blades turn on and off, blinkers work, etc.? |
| OK? | Check out the child locks—do they work well? |
| OK? | Turn the vehicle on, and check the exhaust. Is it clear, rather than white or blue with smoke? Smoke can be a real sign of trouble, indicating oil burning issues, a ring job problem that will be expensive to fix, or possibly even a cracked block, which is a very costly problem that can mean having to replace the engine. In states that have emissions tests, you might not even be able to get the car properly certified to drive if the emissions aren't clean enough. On a cold day, a little white cloudiness when the car first starts is fine—that's probably steam from water vapor. Steam is perfectly normal until the engine warms up. But after the car is warm, the emissions should be colorless. |

## New Cars Only

| | |
|---|---|
| OK? | Make sure all of the appropriate manuals are in the car. |

## Used Cars Only

| | |
|---|---|
| OK? | Check to see if the tires match. Are they all the same size and make? Be sure the numbers on the tire wall are the same. If they don't match, it could mean that the car has issues that wear out tires unevenly, like a bent frame or alignment trouble. It could also mean that the tire suffered a puncture wound or was part of an accident. But these things should have been discussed with the seller, so you should know about them by the time you inspect the vehicle. If the tires don't match, and you don't know why, start asking questions! |
| OK? | Check to be sure all the body panels are roughly the same age and paint color. Can you feel a difference in the paint quality as you run your hands along the panels? If something doesn't feel or look right, the vehicle has probably been in an accident in its past. You should see something about this on a Carfax report, but it may not show up if the owner didn't file a police report. If you feel something bogus, be wary. |
| OK? | Make sure that the spare tire is available and in good condition. Check its pressure. Is it holding pressure? FYI, if it's a small emergency tire, the recommended pressure is likely to be much higher than the standard tire pressure. |
| OK? | Make sure the jack is in the vehicle, all parts are included, and it is in good shape. |
| OK? | Make sure the lug wrench is in the car and that it fits the lug nuts on the vehicle. |
| OK? | Using the hand mirror and flashlight, check inside the wheel wells, along the bottoms of the doors, under the trunk, and all along the chassis, looking for metal stress, rust, suspicious holes, or crumpling. Any of these can indicate a previous wreck, invisible wear-and-tear, or other trouble. |
| OK? | Make sure the gas cap is easy to open and close, fits properly, and if it locks, that the key is available and functional. Ask for any spare keys. |
| OK? | Look very carefully at the condition of the car's carpet. If it's old, it can reveal a whole lot about the life of the car. New carpet isn't always a good sign either. It may be covering up a variety of serious problems, so if it's possible, look underneath it for rust, suspicious stains, or other trouble signs. If it's not possible, be sure to use your hand mirror to take a good look at the floor beneath the passenger cabin for signs of trouble, like rust, holes, and thin spots in the metal. |

Having fun with my friends Jarred and Lou on *Powerblock*.

# SAFETY FIRST!

**R**egardless of the ride you are purchasing, one common denominator applies: the need for safety. Because you are going to depend on your daily driver to keep you protected while on the road, it's essential to weigh vehicle safety standards and features into your purchase decision. It isn't necessarily your own driving that must concern you (or maybe it should!), but that of the others on the road. You want to be as protected as possible in the event of a collision, and therefore I urge you to review government and insurance company crash test ratings for any vehicle you're considering and look into the stock and available add-on safety features before signing your lease or purchase agreement.

More than ever auto manufacturers are considering safety when designing vehicles. Many years ago, when the Insurance Institute for Highway Safety first decided to wreck samples from each car manufacturer's automotive lines to see how the vehicles held up during crashes, only half of those tested managed to get a passable score. Today, almost all vehicles score well in frontal crash testing. There wasn't a single "poor" rating in the most recent round of tests. This is because automotive engineers have developed much stronger and more effective crumple zones, bumpers, and airbags.

Side impact crash test results vary widely among vehicles, as side airbags are still mostly an optional feature. Side airbags, which can mean the difference between life and death in a "T-Bone crash," come stock in most luxury and sports cars. If you can afford to get side airbags in your ride, I believe it's a worthwhile investment in your own safety.

Vehicle rollovers happen most commonly in SUVs and vans and are the cause of nearly a third of all traffic-related deaths. Test results for rollovers also vary widely depending on the make and model. Electronic stability control helps to prevent rollovers, but it doesn't come stock in every vehicle. Find out if the ESC feature is standard or available as an option in the vehicle you are considering, particularly if the prospective ride is an SUV or a van. If you can afford it I definitely suggest getting it.

When reviewing a vehicle's safety statistics, be sure to make note of which safety features were found on that particular car or truck. For instance, if the vehicle that was tested had side airbags and the one you're looking at does not, the results will not be accurate.

Safety tests are conducted annually for all vehicles, the most famous testing facilities being the Insurance Institute for Highway Safety (www.iihs.org), and the National Highway Traffic Safety Administration (www.nhtsa.gov). These websites are fabulous sources for locating information about all vehicles, new or old. The information and statistics they offer goes well beyond crash test ratings. They provide a full data bank listing all recall notices on every make and model, ratings for child car seats, and other useful information and safety data as well.

The organizations conducting the safety tests each use a different system to relay their information. For example, the NHTSA uses a rating system of zero to five stars, with five being the best, while the IIHS gives ratings ranging from Good to Poor. Both convey the same information.

I highly recommend reviewing all safety statistics and features for the vehicle you are considering buying. You and your ride are likely to be together for a long time. Driving a solid car or truck equipped with safety features will help protect you and bring you peace of mind.

## Getting Insured

Yes, it's a pain to have to fork over additional money monthly or quarterly for your insurance premium. But you and your ride deserve to be protected, and you'll be extremely grateful in the event of an accident.

Before choosing an auto insurance provider, research the various companies and rates carefully. There are many options out there. Your insurance payment is going to depend largely on your driving record, the type of vehicle you own, the deductible you choose and where you live. Typical rates in L.A. can vary from less than $100 a month for a two-door Saturn to several hundred if you're driving a high-performance sports car like a Lamborghini. If you insure a vehicle in New York City, the rates will be significantly higher.

You'll want to try not to accumulate points on your driving record. In most states, points are assessed when you receive citations for speeding or other traffic violations, and they will generally raise your insurance rate.

Another factor that will increase your insurance rate is the number of accidents your vehicle has been involved in that you claimed. After an accident, you have the choice to either take care of the damages with the driver outside of your insurance company or involve them to help cover the repairs. If they help cover the costs, you will be responsible for whatever deductible is included in your agreement, and more than likely your insurance rate will go up. The only time you might not want to file a claim with an insurance company after an accident is if it's a minor collision, and the damages are less than or not much more than your deductible. By handling the damages outside of the insurance company, you prevent the downside of an inflated rate.

Please drive safely and hope that whoever is responsible for damage to your vehicle has insurance to cover it.

I use a great insurance provider that has covered the damage caused by two of the hit-and-run accidents to my T-Bird this year. Many plans will cover one or two hit-and-run accidents during the life of the plan. My provider has been extremely fair, accommodating, and professional during our four-year relationship. Make sure you're putting your vehicle in the hands of a strong and reputable company. Car insurance is like health insurance. It's definitely worth researching well and possibly paying a slightly higher premium to get the quality package and professional care you and your ride need and deserve. Also, if you are a student with a B average or better, certain insurance companies will offer a discount. This is one great incentive to do well in school!

## An Important Insurance Caution

Do not let anyone who isn't fully insured drive your vehicle!!! Not only would you and your insurance carrier be responsible for any damage this driver caused, but you would also be responsible for any injury that occurred as a result of the accident. If the driver happened to injure or even kill someone in the collision, and the driver didn't have insurance, you could be slapped with thousands or millions of dollars in lawsuits because he or she was driving your vehicle. It simply isn't worth it. No matter how much your friends or relatives beg you, just say no to uninsured drivers!

The '69 Camaro is one of my favorites.

# HOT CARS, TRUCKS, AND SUVs

*T*here is a multitude of incredible vehicles on the market, and they appeal to each of us for different reasons. It was pretty difficult to narrow down my personal choices to those in this chapter. But to help you with your car shopping I did extensive research and test driving for you, and I have provided an overview of a diverse selection of popular cars, trucks, wagons, SUVs, and minivans that fall into a variety of price ranges. All of the manufacturers on this list have a longstanding reputation in the automotive world, and the majority of the models have received accolades and high ratings over the past few years in categories such as safety, engine performance, and resale value. I've found that all of the rides that I've been impressed by over the years have only gotten better and more advanced in body styling, safety standards, and performance over time. So, unless a vehicle on this list is discontinued, chances are the same model will be as good or better years from now than it is today. Remember, although I personally enjoy the rides on this list and have done thorough research to make sure my opinions are backed by reputable automotive magazines and popular Internet sites such as Edmunds.com and

ConsumerReports.com, only you know what is best for you. I hope this information helps you in your search for the perfect ride!

Before we get started, let's define some of the terms you'll come across as you read this chapter.

- *Continuously Variable Transmission:* Unlike typical automatic transmissions that permit only a small number of gear ratios, CVT is a type of automatic transmission that allows the gear ratio to change to a random, continuous variety of settings within a given range. This allows for an infinite number of possible ratios.
- *MSRP:* Manufacturer's Suggested Retail Price
- *Electronic Stability Control:* ESC helps drivers maintain control in potential skid or slip situations. It does this by sensing which wheels have a problem and then braking or reducing engine power to the specific wheel as needed to help correct the problem.
- *Variable Valve Timing and Electronic Lift Control:* VTEC is a system developed by Honda to increase combustion efficiency in an engine.
- *Advanced Technology Partial Zero-Emission Vehicle:* AT-PZEV is one of the categories of low emissions vehicles in the state of California.
- *Crossover vehicles:* Crossovers are basically compact SUVs. They are built on a car chassis but have four doors and more passenger room and cargo space than a passenger car.

Ok, let's get started! You don't have to give up style just because your budget's a little tight. The following vehicles are extremely economical but they are also stylish. They meet safety standards and get excellent fuel efficiency, which means they save you money and are environmentally friendly. Their price tags are $15,000 or less.

- **Honda Fit** The Fit, with a base MSRP under $14,000, is a fun-to-drive compact car. It has a 109 horsepower 1.5-liter VTEC engine that boasts solid fuel efficiency, getting more than 30 miles per gallon in both the automatic and manual versions. Although it has a compact body style, the interior is adjustable, enabling you to fold seats down to make more room, and there are lots of interior storage compartments. Other features include antilock brakes, a nice audio system, and safety features like front and side curtain airbags. Crank the tunes and enjoy the drive!

- **Ford Focus** Starting at just over $14,000, the two-door coupe has all new sheet metal and a 2.0-liter Duratec 4-cyl engine that puts out 130 horsepower and gets a hefty 37 miles per gallon on the highway. It also has side curtain air bags and standard stability control for safer driving. Ford offers an appealing five-year or 100,000-mile powertrain insurance plan that includes roadside assistance and is transferable between owners. The four-door ST version has a 2.3-liter Duratec engine that puts out an impressive 151 horsepower. And features like the 16-inch alloy wheels, low-profile tires, and sport bucket seats make it look sporty and cool. The Focus is fun to drive and is very well priced.

- **Pontiac G5** At just over $15,000, the G5 coupe is a fun car with an awesome body style that hits the mark in all categories. It has an Ecotec 2.2-liter 4-cylinder engine that puts out 148 horses and gets 34 miles per gallon on the highway. It comes with an MP3 compatible audio system, an optional XM satellite radio, and OnStar with voice navigation. The powertrain warranty is a nice five-year or 100,000-mile plan, and the complete vehicle has a three-year or 36,000-mile warranty. There is also a souped up GT version for a couple thousand more. Love that idea!

- **Chevy Cobalt** The Cobalt is offered in eight hip body styles from a two-door coupe to a full-size sedan, four of the eight falling under $15,000. The power has been increased in comparison to Cobalts of the past with the Ecotec engines, which offer 148–205 horses, depending on which one you choose. The LS Coupe gets a strong 34 miles per gallon on the highway. The audio system is iPod-compatible, which is a great, modern feature. And there are performance-boosting packages available for those who want to beef up the power!

- **VW Rabbit** The Rabbit always had a cute body style, but I feel the new models look even hipper. The Rabbit falls just under $15,000 and is the ideal vehicle for city driving. The 2-door model has a 2.5L engine that puts out a solid 150 horses. It has dual front and side curtain airbags that helped it earn award-winning crash performance safety results. It was also ranked number one in *Car & Driver* magazine. For an extra couple thousand dollars, the 4-door model comes with a 150-horse 2.5-liter engine and many more cool features.

- **Hyundai Accent GLS** The Accent GLS made Edmunds.com's Editor's Most Wanted Vehicles list. With a base price under $13,000, it has a 110-horsepower 1.6-liter 4-cylinder engine that gets an impressive 35 miles per gallon on the highway. This economical car accelerates and handles well and will comfortably carry five adults, making it an advantage for families and the college crowd. Styling has been improved over past models, and now there is a 1.4-liter hybrid version available, which boasts even better fuel economy. One of the best things about the Accent is its five-year or 60,000-mile basic warranty and ten-year or 100,000-mile drivetrain warranty.

- **Nissan Versa**  Versa is short for "versatile," so the sporty Versa sedan, which is powered by a 1.8-liter 4-cylinder engine that delivers 122 horsepower, has a roomy interior and offers a solid amount of cargo space. It gets a commendable 33 average miles per gallon on the highway, and there is also a hatchback version. Cool options like a keyless entry system, Bluetooth Hands-Free Phone System and Continuously Variable Transmission are available. The Versa has many safety features, an attractive exterior design, and it performs and handles well. And above all, at just over $12,000, the price is right.

- **Toyota Yaris**  The Yaris is available in the less expensive Liftback model, which starts under $13,000, or the sedan, which has a five-door layout and a decent amount of interior space. It offers fantastic fuel economy, getting 39 miles per gallon on the highway. It has an MP3 player option with a solid sound system, perfect for cranking your favorite tunes. And the body styling has some punch. Toyotas also have a well-deserved reputation for being very reliable.

- **Kia Rio 5SX**  The Rio 5SX was named one of Edmunds.com's Editors' Most Wanted Vehicles. With a base price of just over $14,000, the Rio and Rio 5 were also the highest ranked sub-compact car in initial quality by J.D. Power & Associates in 2006. The cute Rio 5 has 15-inch tires with alloy wheels, a solid audio system with four speakers, and a ton of safety features, including six airbags, excellent crumple zones in both front and back, and strong, well-engineered side door beams. It also comes with the standard Kia guarantee: ten years or 100,000 miles on the powertrain and five years or 60,000 miles of roadside assistance. This is the perfect car for city driving and those who want an economical ride!

- **Dodge Caliber SE**  Starting around $14,000, the Caliber offers a significant amount for the price tag. It's a 1.8-liter 4-cylinder, and I especially like its electronically controlled all-wheel drive system and its Continuously Variable Transmission, which makes for a smooth, comfortable drive. Having received the highest five-star rating in frontal and side-impact crash tests by the National Highway Traffic Safety Administration (NHTSA), it's a safe vehicle, and Edmunds.com named it one of the Lowest True Cost to Own Vehicles.

- **Jeep Compass**  It's priced slightly higher than $15,000, but this is a sport SUV, so you're getting a lot of vehicle for your dollar. It also has cool styling and road presence. The Compass, with a roomy interior and great-looking exterior design, is a versatile ride that is appropriate for a day of shopping or a night out with friends. It's fuel efficient and has many safety features, such as electronic stability control, antilock brakes, crush zones, and traction control for better road grip. It has a built in tire-pressure monitoring system, and it earned a five-star rating in side-impact crash testing. The Compass is the perfect Jeep model for daily driving.

- **Suzuki SX4**  For a little over a thousand dollars over the base MSRP of $15,500, get the fun, new sport crossover that comes with standard all-wheel drive and gives it the only 3-

mode intelligent all-wheel drive in the class. With a 2.0-liter engine that puts out 143 horsepower, it's pretty powerful. Antilock brakes, Electronic Stability Control, and side curtain airbags are nice standard safety features. It has 16-inch alloy wheels, foldable rear seats for added interior space, and other nice features like a remote keyless entry with a panic button and steering-wheel-integrated audio controls. The SX4 Sport brings the price up very slightly and offers a whole lot more.

The following rides are slightly more expensive, but they offer upgraded styling, performance, and safety standards. These vehicles are still priced below $30,000, some of them falling far below $30,000. You can turn heads without spending a fortune!

- **Toyota Camry Solara** Motor Trend named the Toyota Camry Car of the Year for 2007. The award went to the entire Camry lineup, including the hybrid version, which is the model I'd want to take home. Solara is offered in six sporty models starting at just over $19,000. The SLE Coupe is priced just over $23,000. It's roomy and has an awesome-looking body design. The 2.4-liter four-cylinder model gets 155 horsepower, or a 3.3-liter V6 is available to add an extra 55 horses. The V6 model brings with it Vehicle Stability Control and Traction Control for better handling and safer driving. The Solara has a kicking audio system, multiple air bags and safety features, and gets solid fuel economy. It's the ideal vehicle for almost any lifestyle. If you live where the weather is beautiful, go for the convertible!

- **Mitsubishi Eclipse** The Eclipse's body design is sleek and well contoured. It's available in six sporty models starting at just over $19,000. The GT version comes with a bigger 3.8-liter V-6 engine that boasts an incredible 263 horses. The six-speed manual transmission makes for serious driving! You can feel safer with six airbags, and a performance-tuned suspension system helps it to handle beautifully. It has a solid auto system for cranking the tunes & enjoying your experience on the road. The Eclipse is a hot driving machine!

- **Mazda 6** With a base MSRP of about $19,000, the 6 made Edmunds.com's Editor's Most Wanted Vehicles list. It is extremely affordable, comfortable, and well designed. The 2.3-liter 4-cylinder puts out 156 horses and gets 31 miles per gallon on the highway. It has a sport performance suspension and standard safety features including antilock brakes, traction control, and side curtain airbags. This is an enjoyable car to drive. It's also available in a sport version, a sport wagon, and the Mazda Speed6, which kicks out 270 horsepower. If you like power, I think the Speed6 is calling your name!

- **Toyota Prius** The Prius, with a base MSRP of just over $22,000, is the most popular hybrid on the road. With an EPA-estimated combined city and highway average of 55 miles per gallon and an Advanced Technology Partial Zero Emission Vehicle rating (AT-PZEV), the fuel economy is exceptional. It gets better gas mileage than any five-passenger vehicle on the market. This stylish, four-wheel drive car has a roomy interior and cool available features like Bluetooth wireless technology, a Smart Key system, and a camera to help you when backing up. Also enticing is the fact that if you purchase the Prius you may be entitled to Federal tax benefits. Choosing to drive a vehicle like this with lower fuel emissions also does a great service to our precious environment. I love this car!

- **Honda Civic Hybrid**  In 2006, the Honda Civic sedan was named Motor Trend's Car of the Year. It was also named one of Edmunds.com's Editors' Most Wanted Vehicles. Starting above $22,000, the Civic Hybrid is a green Advanced Technology Partial Zero-Emission Vehicle (AT-PZEV), which makes for another environmentally conscious ride. With this car you definitely ride in style and save yourself tons on fuel costs, while being kind to our environment. The Civic's battery pack comes with an incredible eight-year or 80,000-mile warranty. I also dig its cool, two-tier instrument panel and available navigation system. It's clear why the Civic is an award-winning car!

- **Honda Accord Hybrid**  Starting around $20,000, the Accord is available in a coupe or sedan, and both of those come in a non-hybrid version as well. I recommend the Hybrid sedan version, which offers more room and is just over $31,000 for the base model. It has a beautiful body style and a comfortable, spacious interior. And for those who need speed, the V-6 engine puts out a hefty 253 horsepower! It handles well and gets excellent fuel economy. Again, it pays to be green and makes our environment and those who treasure it very happy!

- **Subaru Impreza WRX**  Subaru has a big line-up of models. The Impreza WRX sedan, starting at just below $24,000, is stylish and comfortable, and-with its 2.5-liter intercooled, supercharged engine putting out a significant 224 horses-it performs well. It has an upgraded, six-speaker audio system including MP3/WMA CD playback and SIRIUS Satellite

Radio capability. It's all-time four-wheel drive, and it still gets a decent 26 miles per gallon on the highway. The interior of the WRX has a new steering wheel and cool performance-design front seats. Subaru is of course famous for their practical and reliable wagons. The WRX wagon is a terrific choice as well.

- **Mercury Montego**  The Montego is a spacious, front-wheel drive sedan with a nice body design and a lot of interior room and trunk space. It was awarded the Best in Class Ideal Vehicle Award from AutoPacific, and it earned the government's highest five-star front crash test rating three years in a row. The engine is a 3.0-liter V6 that gets a solid 203 miles per gallon, and the car offers decent fuel economy with an estimated 29 miles per gallon on the highway. The base MSRP is under $25,000, which isn't bad for all you're getting with this comfortable, reliable sedan.

- **Nissan Altima**  The Altima SE sedan starts at $24,000 and with its 3.5-liter V6 engine, puts out an impressive 250 horsepower. It has a bold body design and 17-inch aluminum alloy wheels. With a sport-tuned suspension it's agile on the road and has solid fuel efficiency, and with its Continuously Variable Transmission, traction control, and an antilock braking system, the car grips the road well and is safe to drive. It also has features like heated outside mirrors with turn signal indicators, a fancy push-button ignition, and a touch-screen navigation system. This is a terrific daily driver.

- **Nissan Maxima**  The Maxima, starting around $28,000, is a great-looking sedan that offers exhilarating performance. It has a roomy, comfortable interior. The Continuously Variable Transmission makes for a better driving experience, and the

3.5-liter V6 engine kicks out 255 horsepower. I especially like the body design, 17-inch alloy wheels, and the skyview glass-paneled roof. The Maxima also has an Intelligent Key system and fancy High Intensity Discharge bi-xenon headlights, which makes both high and low beams much higher than with halogen bulbs.

- **Acura TSX**  The TSX, starting at just over $28,000, is a sporty, yet elegant sedan—a perfect combination. It has a 2.4-liter, four-cylinder engine boasting 205 horsepower and a double-wishbone suspension system and Vehicle Stability Assist superior handling and control. The TSX really hugs the road and is fun to drive. The automatic version gets an estimated 31 miles per gallon on the highway. Safety features include antilock brakes, crumple zones, and front and side curtain airbags. It has a premium audio system and an available navigation system.

- **Ford Fusion**  With a base price of approximately $18,000, the Fusion is a hip, sporty midsize sedan that comes with cool halogen headlamps and three different engine options. The cast aluminum engine block, aluminum cylinder heads, and rack and pinion power steering help make it lighter and more fun to drive. J.D. Power and Associates named it the Most Appealing Vehicle in 2006. It has a 2.3-liter 4-valve per cylinder engine that delivers 160 horses and gets a considerable 31 miles per gallon on the highway. Other key features are an anti-theft perimeter alarm system and front airbags and side-impact air curtains. It's quick, stylish and comfortable. It also comes in an enticing all-wheel drive version. A couple of years ago Ford gave me the "Ford Fusion: Life in Drive Award," which was a huge honor. And in 2006 the Fusion became Ford Racing's official racecar for NASCAR.

- **Hyundai Azera**  The Azera sedan, with a base price of approximately $27,000, was named one of Edmunds.com's Editor's Most Wanted Vehicles. The 3.8-liter V6 kicks out a big 263 horses, making it the fastest Hyundai in history. This front-wheel drive sedan has a plush, roomy interior and is a smooth car to drive. It has many impressive features, such as a tire pressure monitor and turn signal indicators in the side-view mirrors. Some of the optional features, still bringing the price in under $30,000, are leather interior, heated seats, traction/stability controls, eight airbags, a more gutsy V8 engine, and fancier wheels. That is a phenomenal price for all you get with the Azera.

- **Chevy Impala**  The Impala comes in many styles. The LTZ starts just above $27,000 and offers a lot for a reasonable pricetag. The sedan comfortably seats six, and with exterior features like foglamps, a rear spoiler, and dual stainless steel exhaust tips, it looks cool on the road. The 3.9-liter V6 with Variable Valve Timing gets 233 horses and comes with GM's Active Fuel Management System, which shuts off half of the cylinders when full power isn't needed, which means improved fuel economy and money saved. The same system is available on the V-8 engine SS model. Other great features on the LTZ are Onstar, a kicking Bose sound system with an auxiliary input jack for iPod or MP3 devices, and a remote vehicle starter system.

- **Buick Lucerne CX**  The elegant Lucerne sedan has road presence and handles well. It also offers power and decent fuel economy with its 3.8- liter V-6 that puts out around 200 horses and gets 28 miles per gallon in highway driving. The Lucerne earned five stars in the U.S. Government's Frontal

NCAP test. It also comes with a strong powertrain warranty of 100,000 miles or five years. For the first time in a decade Buick is offering an optional 4.6-liter V8 that boasts 275 horsepower and also gets 28 mpg on the highway. That's quite a lot of power, and it's a remarkably smooth, quiet ride at high speeds.

- **VW Passat**  The Passat's base MSRP is just over $23,000 for the standard model with the 200 horsepower 2.0 T (turbo). During my first few years in Los Angeles I leased the four-cylinder Passat, and it made for the ideal daily driver. I prefer the version that comes with a 3.6-liter V6 that puts out 280 horses and goes for just over $30,000. I enjoy the way this mid-size sedan handles and performs. And I love the body design and high-tech instrument panel. The Passat is roomy and comfortable and received excellent crash test ratings. With models priced below $30,000, it's an all around great car for a fair price. It's also available in a wagon version, and remember, wagons are hot right now!

- **Chrysler 300**  Motor Trend named the Chrysler 300 Car of the Year in 2005. With a base MSRP of approximately $25,000, the Chrysler 300 is a sexy, sophisticated sedan that has impeccable styling. It really exudes power on the road. The standard engine is a 2.7-liter V6 putting out 190 horses. But for a few thousand more, the 300C version comes with the powerful 5.7-liter V8 boasting a hefty 340 horses! I thoroughly enjoyed my test drive and thought the 300 handled amazingly and had exceptional acceleration. The sedan has an especially long wheelbase, making for a spacious interior, and the silver accents and old-school analog clock add to the car's elegant feel.

- **Lincoln Zephyr/MKZ** Formerly the Zephyr, the MKZ is a beautiful, all-wheel drive sedan with a V6 engine that puts out 263 horses. The MKZ, with a base price of just under $30,000, has earned a few accolades. It was voted "Best Luxury Car Interior" by automotive journalists, was named one of Ward's 10 Best Engines and was voted Best Audio System by CNET.com. Its available MP3-compatible THX II Certified Car Audio System is one of the best on the market, putting out 600 watts through fourteen speakers. It also has the Intelligent All-Wheel Drive System, which senses and helps counteract wheel spin, allowing the car to grip the road better. It has a spacious backseat and is a comfortable ride that maneuvers well. I also love Lincoln's MKR!

- **Dodge Charger R/T** Built tough enough to be used as a police car, the Charger is strong and reliable and has a comfortable, spacious interior. The R/T version starts around $32,000 and comes with that famous Dodge HEMI V8 engine which puts out a hefty 340 horses! The R/T's 5.7-liter HEMI was named one of Ward's 10 Best Engines for 2006. The 2007 Charger earned the government's highest possible five-star front crash-test rating. And it has earned other awards including those for interior design, safety standards, and exterior design. It accelerates and brakes impressively and is an all around quality ride. You can get the less "muscular" model for a bit less money, but I think it's better with that awesome HEMI.

- **Mustang GT** The Mustang GT represents legendary muscle. Mustangs have true muscle car roots and have always been stylish and strong in the performance category. The Mustang GT Deluxe coupe, starting around $26,000, has a 4.6-liter V8 engine that kicks out an impressive 300 horsepower. It also received solid crash test ratings for both front and side impact, and it has an antilock braking system and traction control for better road grip. Exterior features include a forward-leaning egg crate grille, cool 17-inch cast aluminum wheels, and halogen headlamps. The manual version gets decent fuel economy at 25 miles per gallon on the highway, and with a sports car like this, the manual is much more fun. This is a killer looking ride. If you want to spend additional money, this is also a perfect car to lower and trick out. Mustangs have a sea of devoted fans, so it should be easy to find a local Mustang Club to share hot ideas for customizing and beefing up its performance.

- **Audi A3**  Starting at just over $23,000, the A3 is a sporty four-door wagon that offers both luxury and practicality. It's stylish and comfortable and performs well with its six-speed 2.0 T V6 with an exhaust turbocharger that puts out a strong 200 horsepower and gets 32 miles per gallon on the highway. A few of the other cool features are 17-inch alloy wheels, an advanced anti-theft alarm system, a brake pad wear indicator, and dual climate control air conditioning. This is a really solid, practical ride for daily driving.

- **Dodge Magnum**  The Magnum was named one of Edmunds.com's Editors' Most Wanted Vehicles. The standard SE model starts at a base price of around $24,000 and is equipped with a 2.7-liter 24-valve V6 engine kicking out 190 horses. Folding seats give it more than 70 feet of cargo space, and it has power four-wheel disc brakes. For a little more than $32,000, you can get the R/T model. The R/T's 5.7-liter 340-horse HEMI was named one of Ward's 10 Best Engines in 2007. The R/T model also has 18-inch machined aluminum wheels, Electronic Stability Control with all-speed Traction Control for better braking power and road grip, stylish leather trimmed seats, and a 276-watt sound system with six speakers. This is a very cool wagon for a variety of lifestyles.

- **Mazda RX-8** The RX-8's styling and engine make it a true sports car. Mazda calls this sports car a "speed machine." The Sport version starts at just over $27,000 and comes with a 1.3-liter Renesis 2-rotor rotary engine that gives it 212 horsepower. It has a gorgeous interior and unique freestyle rear doors, which open toward the front of the car and give the illusion of a 2-door vehicle. Other cool features are a tire pressure monitoring system, alarm system with an engine immobilizer, and remote keyless illuminated entry. The RX-8 performs beautifully and handles well, and the 6-speed automatic transmission with paddle shifters helps make it a blast to drive!

- **Mini Cooper S** The adorable Mini made Edmunds.com's Editors' Most Wanted Vehicles list. The Mini, with an MSRP base price of around $22,000, has a 172-horsepower turbocharged 16-valve alloy engine that gets an impressive 36 miles per gallon on the highway in the automatic version. I like its stance on the road and think it looks incredibly stylish with the racing stripes! Other Mini features are 16-inch alloy wheels with run-flats, six airbags with side protection, and oversized brakes in front for optimal braking. Yes it's cute, but it's also powerful and agile on the road. I had some serious fun with my dad in the S model while at the Lime Rock racetrack in Connecticut. I actually scared him when I

**What's all of the fuss about child car seats and the way they are supposed to be strapped into the vehicle?**

Listen to this statistic: 90 percent of children under five years of age that are killed in automobile accidents would have survived had they been properly strapped into child car seats. Seat belts alone don't work for small children. Children can easily slip out of adult seat belts, or the belts could injure them on impact. A child could also be knocked out of an adult's arms on impact, so holding a child while a car is in motion is never safe.

Child safety seats are designed to accommodate children by weight, not age. By law, car seats are supposed to be properly strapped with seat belts into the backseats of the vehicle. For infants, safety seats are required to face backward to prevent whiplash and flying glass in the event that the vehicle stops abruptly or is involved in a collision. Please review and obey your state laws.

After a child has outgrown the safety seat (again, check your state laws for weight limits), he or she is safe to ride shotgun, but he or she must always wear a seat belt.

And *please* do not ever leave children alone in a vehicle. There have been countless tragedies due to parental irresponsibility and neglect. Kids have accidentally slipped cars out of gear and rolled them into oncoming traffic, started cars and driven them into traffic, and, most frequently, have been injured or killed by the heat trapped in parked cars. We also need to be aware of our pets. Pets left unsupervised in hot cars are also at risk for heat injuries or death.

**I'm a woman. Can you give me tips on parking safely in a large lot and avoiding danger?**

Park close to the front door of a building or home whenever possible. Park where the street or lot is well lit. Don't ever park next to a van. If you're alone and feel unsafe, wait for other people to be within your vicinity before walking to your ride. Always move quickly with your keys in your hand, and lock your doors immediately after getting inside your vehicle. I usually call a friend if it's late and I'm alone, inform them where I am and ask them to stay on the phone with me until I'm safe. If you're really nervous, ask a security guard or police officer to walk you to your vehicle. I've done it many times.

got it up to high speeds! Unsurprisingly, this little car is a champion at holding its resale value. It's also unexpectedly roomy inside. And the Mini will fit in pretty much any compact parking space, so it's the perfect car for city driving. There is also a hot S convertible for several thousand more.

- **Chrysler Sebring**  Starting at around $19,000, the Sebring has a nice body style, a comfortable interior, and it handles well. It has electronic stability control, front and side curtain air bags, a tire pressure monitoring system, and it received the highest government frontal crash test rating of five stars, so it's also a safe ride. With its standard 2.4-liter 4-cylinder DOHC engine gets an average of 32 mpg on highway and puts out 173 horses. It also comes in a 2.7-liter V6 engine or a 3.5-liter V6. There is a range of luxurious interior options for all models.

- **Mazda MX-5 Miata**  Mazda recently brought their sporty roadster back to America. The Miata was originally a flashy concept car, but its overwhelming appeal turned it into a popular production vehicle. And, at a base MSRP of just over $21,000, it's fairly priced for all you get with the car. The six-speed manual transmission allows for fun driving, and it handles well, boasts precise rack-and-pinion steering, and has a solid suspension system. Its manual convertible top is easy to maneuver, and there is an optional power hard top available in the '07 model as well. It's obvious why *Car & Driver* rated the MX-5 one of the 10 Best Cars of 2007 and Edmunds.com named it a Most Wanted Vehicle.

- **Pontiac Solstice**  The Solstice, with a base MSRP of just over $22,000, is a flashy two-seater that has attitude and offers some solid power. The stock version puts out 177 horsepower and gets 28 miles per gallon on the highway, and you can upgrade to a 260-horsepower 2.0 liter turbo manual version that gets an estimated 31 miles per gallon on the highway. The Ecotec engine produces more power, while consuming less fuel. The suspension system is also strong, featuring Coil-Over Bilstein Monotube Shocks. It has a five-year or 100,000-mile warranty on the powertrain and a three-year or 36,000-mile warranty on the entire vehicle. Driving the Solstice is an absolute blast!

- **Honda S2000** Starting at just over $34,000, this hot roadster turns heads and boasts power, with its 237-horsepower 2.2-liter Variable Valve Timing and Lift Electronic Control (VTEC) engine. The Honda 2000 designers took into account Honda's success throughout several decades in the racing world, particularly recently on the Indy circuit, and incorporated the double wishbone suspension and coil springs to emulate that fabulous handling found in racecars. The suspension system makes it the perfect car for the road or the track. And the body style is hot! Other key features are light-weight alloy wheels, high-intensity discharge headlights, decent storage space, electronically powered soft top, and a powerful audio system with eight speakers.

- **Saturn Sky** The Sky, priced just above $25,000 for the standard model, has a sharp, stylish body design. This is another hot roadster. It's also fast and powerful, so for all of this, the price is very fair. Many magazines and auto publications have raved about the Sky convertible. Its 16-valve engine puts out 177 horses and has Variable Valve Timing, which maximizes the power the engine can generate. The fuel economy is an estimated 28 miles per gallon on the highway. Some great features include Onstar, a security system and engine immobilizer, dual-stage front airbags (which deploy in two stages based on severity of the impact), rear-wheel drive, and a solid suspension system. This car rocks! It will go from zero to sixty in approximately seven seconds, and it hugs the road beautifully.

These coupes, sedans, and wagons are upwards of $30,000 for those with bigger budgets . . . some are over $40,000. But these are many of the top rides on the market, and I feel their attributes justify their price tags.

- **Infiniti G35**  Motor Trend chose the G35 as car of the year for 2003. It's referred to as a sedan/coupe combo. The G35 also made Edmunds.com's Editors' Most Wanted Vehicles list. With a base price of just over $31,000, all models have the 3.5-liter V-6 engine that kicks out an impressive 306 horsepower! The G35's six-speaker Infiniti Studio on Wheels by Bose audio system was named one of Ward's Auto World's Best twelve years in a row. Wow, crank the tunes and step on the gas! The driver's seat has 8-way power adjustments with available memory functions, and it has a luxurious leather interior. The G35 also has an available touch screen navigation system, Infiniti Intelligent Key with Push Button Ignition, a dual-stage air bag system and fancy bi-xenon headlamps. It's agile and comfortable and it perfectly blends sportiness and luxury.
- **Lexus ES 350**  The stunning ES 350 is a midsize luxury sedan with a base price of just over $33,000. It is refined and comfortable, and it offers many safety and performance features. The engine is a 3.5-liter V6 with a six-speed automatic trans-

mission that puts out a considerable 272 horses. Some of the interior features of the ES 350 are premium wood, polished metal and leather accents, dual-zone automatic climate control, 10-way power front seats, a sliding center console, and an interior LED soft-lighting system. For safety it has up to 10 airbags, Vehicle Stability Control, Traction Control, a Direct Tire Pressure Monitor, antilock brakes with brake assist, and crumple zones. It was given an Ultra-Low Emissions Vehicle rating, which means the car is easier on the environment, and it has a dual exhaust system for ultimate efficiency and power. If you want luxury, performance, and safety and you also want to be more environmentally friendly, this is your car. Of course you'll have to get it with the panorama roof that has a fixed glass panel over the rear-seat area and a sliding sunroof over the front seats!

- **Mercedes-Benz C-Class** The C-Class is a line of luxurious and sporty sedans starting just above $30,000. I like them all, but if I was going to drive one I'd go for the C350 sport sedan. It all depends on your needs. The C350 has a powerful 268-horsepower V6 engine with various transmission options. It carries five and gets an average of 28 miles per gallon on the highway. It handles incredibly and is a comfortable ride. It also received excellent scores in crash tests. The base model with the 2.5-liter V6 engine puts out upwards of 200 horses, while the top of the line 5.5-liter V8 engine kicks out more than 360 horses. If you can afford the few thousand dollars extra, the V8 is the way to go!

- **Jaguar X-Type** The Jaguar X-Type, starting at just under $35,000, has an elegant body design and, although 60 percent of the power makes its way to the rear wheels, the car has full time Traction 4 all-wheel drive handling to help keep it safely on the road. This is one of my very favorite cars to drive and is the epitome of class. Some key exterior features are the distinctive Jaguar grille, signature hood ornament, 16-inch alloy wheels, and four headlamps. And the roomy interior is plush and gorgeous with a standard moonroof, leather seats, and elegant wood and leather touches throughout. The driver has an 8-way power adjustable seat, and there is automatic climate control and a 120-watt audio system. The 3.0-liter V6 delivers 277 horsepower, and the car is agile and comfortable at high speeds. For those who like a wagon, that version is available as well.

- **BMW 3 Series** The 3 Series, perfectly combining a sporty feel with elegance, is on Edmunds.com's Editors' Most Wanted Vehicles list. Both the coupe (starting at a much lower $40,000) and convertible (starting at around $49,000) are nice options. Many years ago I owned a BMW 325i convertible that I bought used. I found it to be beautiful, comfortable, and agile—truly the ultimate driving machine. In my opinion all BMWs look stylish and perform exceptionally, and they've just gotten better over the years. The 335i has a 3.0-liter V6 engine that kicks out a considerable 300 horsepower and gets an average of 28 miles per gallon on the highway. Safety features include standard antilock brakes, Stability Control, traction control and many airbags. The 335i is a blast to drive. The 3 Series also offers sedans, a wagon, and a convertible in their line up.

- **Cadillac CTS** With a base MSRP of just over $30,000, the CTS is a stunning sedan. It comes with GM's 100,000-mile or five-year transferable powertrain warranty with no deductible. For a few thousand more you can get a special edition with an available 3.6-liter V6 engine putting out 300 horses. This model has an available all-wheel drive system, and another very cool feature is the Adaptive Forward Lighting System, which helps when driving at night by automatically steering the headlights. It has a gorgeous hand-crafted interior, and the Bose audio system is equipped with ten speakers. For great sky views, there is a double-sized sunroof covering more than 70 percent of the roof. It's a smooth, quiet ride that offers substantial power and strong acceleration. It's also comfortable and scored well on crash tests. I really dig this car.

- **Audi A4**  Starting at just over $28,000, the A4 series was recently given a "Top Safety Pick" rating by the Insurance Institute for Highway Safety. There is a 200-horsepower 2.0 T turbo engine, and for several thousand more you can upgrade to the four-door sedan with the 255-horsepower 3.2-liter V6 with Continuously Variable Transmission. A heftier V8 engine is available as well. The 4-cylinder gets an estimated 30 miles per gallon, while the V6 gets 29 miles per gallon in city driving. The A4 has a cool body design and a comfortable, stylish interior. This is just a nice, safe, reliable ride. The A4 also comes in a convertible or a wagon version, which made Edmunds.com's Editors's Most Wanted Vehicles list.

- **Ford Shelby GT Mustang**  This car is hot! With a base MSRP of approximately $37,000, the GT kicks out an awesome 319 horses. New shocks and struts lower the ride height, which gives it a sexy stance, and I love that it just defines muscle. It has eighteen-inch wheels and cool low-profile tires and an aluminum hood with a hood scoop. Spend about $42,000 (including a $1,300 gas guzzler tax) for the supercharged GT500 Fastback model, and you can own the fastest production Mustang ever built. If past patterns of Shelby cars are an indicator, this car is going to become another collectible. The GT500 has a supercharged 5.4-liter, 32-valve V8 engine that puts out almost 500 horses. Make sure you can handle all that power! Other bonus features are "Powered by SVT" fitted cam covers, a hot T-56 six-speed transmission, a leather dash, and massive nineteen-inch machined aluminum wheels.

- **BMW 5 Series**  Starting at around $48,000, the 5 Series represents BMW's luxury midsize sedan, a car that has been about the driving experience and killer performance and styling for decades. The 5 Series is safe and quiet and comfortably carries four adults. There are many engine choices available, as well as both manual and automatic transmissions. The 3.0-liter delivers 215 horsepower while the V8 makes a whopping 360! The 5 Series was named one of Edmunds.com's Editors' Most Wanted Vehicles. It also comes with an auxiliary audio input that's compatible with an iPod or other MP3 player, plus and a tire-pressure monitor. A really cool new available feature is the high-definition radio and Night Vision system that uses a thermal-imaging camera to constantly monitor the road. The BMW's iDrive has always been another helpful feature. For those of you who love wagons, there is also a sport wagon version available in the 5 Series as well.

- **Infiniti M35**  At just over $41,000 the M35 is roomy, safe and an excellent combination of luxury and performance. It's a rear-wheel drive sedan with a five-speed automatic transmission and a V6 engine that puts out an awesome 275 horse-power. Its beautiful body style is complimented by stylish 8-spoke 18-inch alloy wheels. This car is well equipped, comfortable, and handles well. It's also available in the all-wheel drive and sport versions. One very cool feature is the available Lane Departure Warning System, which has a camera that monitors the car's position between the highway lines and will inform you if the vehicle drifts too far out of the lane.

- **Volvo Hardtop C70** Volvo has a reputation for constructing beautiful and safe vehicles. At just over $39,000, the C70 convertible (or coupe) has sleek styling, offers key safety features such as inflatable air bar curtains and a roll over protection system, and it performs well. Its five-cylinder turbocharged engine puts out 218 horses. It's a roomy car that comfortably carries four adults and has ample storage and versatility. I especially like the fact that the C70 meets the toughest emissions standards, like California's ULEV II. My sister, Jordyn, used to drive the C70, and I would swap rides with her all of the time so I could drive it. It's one of my very favorite cars.

- **Saab 9-3 Convertible** At a base MSRP of about $37,000, the Saab 9-3 convertible comes with GM's five-year or 100,000-mile powertrain warranty. It has a beautiful, comfortable interior and an available six-CD changer with a Bose Sound System. While the standard engine is a turbocharged 210-horse 2.0-liter, it's also offered in a 2.8-liter 250-horse V6 that gets an estimated 30 miles per gallon in highway driving. Other features are a Traction Control System, 16-inch alloy wheels, electronic stability program, antilock brakes, premium audio system, and an eight-way power driver's seat. The Saab convertible has great ergonomics and solid safety features and is killer to drive. There are also cool wagons and sedans in this series.

Did you know that in the past couple of years SUVs and trucks have outsold passenger cars? Here are some of my favorite trucks and SUVs. The following SUV's cost $25,000 or less:

- **Chevy Equinox** Starting at around $23,000, the Equinox LS has a 3.4-liter V6 engine that delivers 185 horsepower. It comes with electronic stability control, four-wheel antilock disc brakes and received excellent safety ratings. The Equinox is available in all-wheel drive, and it's an especially spacious SUV. With folding rear seats, there is plenty of cargo space and room to comfortably carry a 6.6 foot adult. The folding front passenger seat also makes room for long cargo items. It is reasonably priced, and there is an available 3.5-Liter V6 engine that I like even better!

- **Ford Escape** With an MSRP just below $20,000, the Escape leads the small SUV class in sales. It has power rack-and-pinion steering, MacPherson struts, coil springs, a stabilizer bar, and an available Intelligent 4-Wheel Drive System for an enjoyable ride that feels more like a car than an SUV. One very appealing feature is its updated five-year or 60,000-mile powertrain warranty. The Escape is available in a range of engine options, the V6 delivering 200 horses. It's able to tow up to 3,500 pounds, and a split bench helps make the interior spacious and versatile. For a few additional thousands there is also a hybrid model available, which was the first hybrid SUV on the market. That's the one I'd go with!

- **Toyota Tacoma**  The Tacoma made Edmunds.com's Editors' Most Wanted list. With a base MSRP for the 4x4 of about $19,000, this truck offers quite a bit. The regular cab model comes with a 2.7-liter DOHC 4-cylinder that puts out 159 horsepower. The 4.0-liter 236-horsepower DOHC engine version brings the price tag up to about $25,000, but this is also a double cab, four door, and four-wheel drive truck. The Tacoma is relatively new to the truck world, and with it comes a lot of truck for your buck. The Tacoma has wide-opening doors that make it easier to load cargo in and out. And the various cab formation options allow you to buy a truck with the exact space you will need. The chassis is strong, and the multiple models make it easy to tailor the truck to meet your specifications as well. I dig it!

- **Honda Element**  Starting around $19,000, the Element is the perfect utility vehicle. It has a boxy shape, wide-opening cargo doors, and a clam shell tailgate, which opens both upward and downward. The trunk and adaptable seating configuration allows you to maximize interior space and make room for things like surfboards, bikes, sporting equipment, or wheelchairs. Like all Hondas, the Element is well engineered. It received the highest five-star frontal and side-impact crash test ratings from the NHTSA. My mom drives one. She cares for my disabled aunt, Barbie, and the Element's low chassis makes it easy for Barbie to step in and out of the vehicle, and the low tailgate makes it easy to load her wheelchair into the trunk.

- **Kia Sportage**  With a base MSRP of about $17,000, the Sportage lives up to its name as a sporty compact SUV. It's offered in a 140-horsepower 4-cylinder engine or a 173-

horsepower V6 version, and it's available in front- or all-wheel drive. Safety features include antilock breaks, anti-skid control, and front and side curtain airbags. The EX package comes with leather seats and seat heaters for the front seats, and it has Kia's fantastic ten-year or 100,000-mile limited powertrain warranty and five-year or 60,000-mile limited basic warranty. The Sportage has received a five-star safety rating from the NHTSA, was named one of Edmunds.com's Top 10 Most Fuel Efficient vehicles, and Kelley Blue Book named it one of the Top 10 coolest new cars selling under $18,000. The Sportage is definitely a winner!

- **Toyota Rav4**  The Rav4, with a base MSRP of about $21,000, is referred to as the first crossover vehicle on the market. The interior is versatile, allowing you to create more space and even make room for an optional third-row seat. It's reasonably priced, stylish, smooth, and comfortable. There is the standard 2.4-liter 4-cylinder model that puts out 166 horses, and an available 3.5-liter V6 that produces a significant 269 horses! Both versions boast impressive fuel economy. The Rav4 also comes with a sound system equipped for an MP3 player and has pretty much power everything.

- **Suzuki XL7**  The XL7 front-wheel drive base model starts around $23,000. The XL7 SUV has great styling, available all-wheel drive, and a 3.6-liter DOHC V6 engine that puts out over 250 horses. This five-speed automatic has options including seating for seven, a navigation system, and a rear seat DVD player. It also comes with America's number one warranty: 100,000 miles or seven years, no deductible, fully transferable. Amazing.

- **Hyundai Santa Fe**  With a base MSRP of about $22,000, the

Santa Fe has many standard safety features like electronic stability control, traction control, antilock breaks, and six airbags. It's a versatile ride that accommodates a variety of lifestyles. The Santa Fe offers a 2.7-liter DOHC V6 in the base model and a 3.3-liter V6 in the SE model. For about two thousand additional dollars, the SE version definitely steps it up with many additional features. The Santa Fe has a strong safety record, having been awarded NHTSA's highest five-star crash ratings. It also holds its value extremely well.

- **Jeep Liberty**  Who doesn't love a Jeep? I've been hosting a travel adventure series called *Destination Wild* on Fox Sports Net, and we travel all over the country, tackling all types of terrain in many different Jeep models. They make for the ideal adventure vehicles. The Liberty, with a base MSRP of about $22,000, is rugged and sturdy, and it can handle tough terrain. It has rack-and-pinion steering and a huge 5,000-pound towing capacity. For safety it has electronic stability control and antilock brakes, and it offers available part time four-wheel drive. It's also family friendly, has a nice, spacious interior, and offers many luxury options. Its 3.7-liter V6 gives it some power too!

- **Honda CR-V**  The CR-V crossover, with a base MSRP of just over $20,000, was named one of Edmunds.com's Editors' Most Wanted Vehicles. Its 166-horsepower 2.4-liter DOHC 4-cylinder engine with five-speed automatic transmission offers some solid power. The CR-V was originally built on the Civic platform and quickly became the best-selling compact SUV on the market. Standard safety features include antilock brakes, Vehicle Stability Assist, and traction control, and it was given the NHTSA's highest five-star frontal and side-impact ratings. There are many models and a multitude of cool features and available options.

For some additional dollars, I recommend the following SUVs, compact SUVs/Crossovers, and Trucks :

- **Toyota Highlander Hybrid**  The Highlander is a sophisticated, good-looking midsize SUV that starts at a base price of about $33,000. It delivers some significant power with its 208 horsepower 3.3-liter DOHC V6, and it is also a comfortable, quiet ride that doesn't have the feel of an SUV. The emissions are extremely low, so this is the perfect ride for those who need a roomy vehicle with a lot of cargo space but also want to be environmentally friendly. There are other Highlander models, but the hybrid is the way to go!

- **Honda Pilot**  The Pilot, with a base MSRP of about $27,000, is Honda's midsize SUV with seating for up to eight passengers. It was on *Car & Driver*'s "5 Best Trucks" list six years in a row in the class of large Sport-Utility Vehicles. The Institute for Highway Safety (IIHS) listed the Pilot as a "Top Safety Pick" in 2007. And it was also deemed a "Best Buy" in the midsize SUV category by *Consumer Guide* magazine. The Pilot is also a very safe vehicle, having scored the top five-star rating in NHTSA's frontal and side-impact tests. And it is efficient, practical, and, on top of all of that . . . affordable. I didn't even mention the 244-horse V6 engine, and I bet I already had you sold!

- **The Ford Edge**  Starting around $26,000, the new Edge crossover has a bold body design, a signature Ford grill, and cool halogen headlamps. It's agile, handling like a sports car, and has available all-wheel drive. It also has AdvanceTrak with Roll Stability Control (RSC). It received top scores in the safety department with features like an impact-absorbing body structure, the Safety Canopy System and air bags along the front and sides. It comes with an optional double-paneled Vista Roof, allowing both front and rear passengers panoramic views. The 3.5-liter V6 engine delivers a solid 265 horsepower and decent gas mileage, getting 25 miles per gallon on the highway. The Edge seats five, and the seats can be folded to create additional cargo space. It also has a kicking audio system. The Edge offers a lot for a terrific price.

- **Saturn Vue** The Vue is a compact SUV that has a clean and stylish body design and offers power and a solid 3,500-pound towing capacity. The Vue Green Line hybrid has a base MSRP of about $24,000, and it gets impressive fuel economy. With an estimated 32 highway miles per gallon, it receives better fuel economy than any other Vue and the best of any other SUV out there. GM offers a five-year or 100,000-mile power-train warranty, and there are many safety features on the Vue, including a steel space frame, antilock brakes, a top five-star safety rating, front and side air bags, and a rollover sensing system. There is ample storage space and an available navigation system, and the audio system comes standard with CD and MP3 capability. The 3.5-liter V6 engine kicks out 250 horses, and the 2.4-liter Green Line puts out 170 horsepower. The Vue is a family-friendly and inexpensive SUV. It has a lot of interior room without resembling a school bus, and it's backed with unbeatable service departments at Saturn dealers. Consumer surveys rank Saturn service at the top in the field.

- **GMC Acadia** The Acadia, with a base list price of about $30,000, is considered a crossover SUV. It has seven-passenger seating with an available bench for an eighth passenger, unibody construction, which saves weight and maximizes space, standard six airbags and side airbag curtains, and stabilitrak to help maintain traction on the roads. A few of the other cool features are a tire-pressure monitoring system, dual exhaust with chrome tips, eighteen-inch tires and aluminum wheels, and fog lamps. I especially love the double-panel skyscape roof, which provides exterior sky views and offers lots of light.

- **Chevy Silverado**  The Silverado was named Motor Trend's Truck of the Year for 2007. Chevy has always been on the forefront of safety, and the Silverado has many key safety features, including an antilock break system, Stabilitrak, Traction Control, Onstar, airbags, and a safety cage construction. It has GM's five-year or 100,000-mile Powertrain Limited Warranty. The Silverado handles well, has solid road traction, and has a strong tow capacity. The base model has a Vortec 4.3-liter V6. There is also a 4.8-liter V8, a 5.3-liter V8, a 6.0-liter V8, and for those who can afford the top of the line and need some serious power for towing or off-roading, there is a Duramax Diesel 6.6-liter V8 Turbo! I haven't had a ride in the 6.0 or 6.6 yet. If you buy this truck, call me!

- **Ford Explorer**  The Explorer received five stars in crash test ratings and is a long-running favorite among families and those who need a sturdy vehicle with power and a significant amount of interior space. It comfortably accommodates seven, and the back seats are removable, which makes for more cargo space. The Explorer XLT has a 4.0-liter 6-cylinder that gets an estimated 20 miles per gallon on the highway. It also comes with Ford's powertrain warranty and is available with Sirius Satellite Radio. Ford has redesigned the suspension system and implemented an Intelligent Safety System, so the Explorer is stable and adjusts performance according to your needs. It's a very comfortable ride. Several of my friends own this SUV and have been faithful to it for years.

- **Toyota 4-Runner**  The 4-Runner, starting at a base MSRP of about $28,000, represents practicality and luxury in an SUV. Its engineering is formidable, and it's a great driving machine equipped for just about any terrain. The base model comes with a 4.0-liter DOHC V6, and there is an available 4.7-liter DOHC V8. The 4-Runner has traction control, and the limited slip center differential on the four-wheel drive models keeps this SUV moving on rough ground when other vehicles have to stop. It's also a comfortable SUV that's perfect for large families or the college scene.

- **F-150**  The F-150 is a member of Ford's F-series family, which has been America's best selling truck for the past thirty years! And this pick-up just keeps getting better. It's rugged, with the most cargo box volume of any truck in its class, and it has a towing capacity that surpasses all others. It's reliable, handsome, and comfortable to drive. It can handle rough terrain but is also perfect for daily driving. It seats six and has huge cargo space in the truck bed. The F-150 has solid engine power with several engine variations that allow you to buy the amount of power you need for your lifestyle. The V8 is available in a Flexible Fuel Vehicle version, which will run on gas, Ethanol, or any combo of the two. It also has a Tire Pressure Monitoring System and an entertainment system on the back seats. It's a classic choice for style, dependability, and attitude. I would personally go with the 2008 version designed by Chip Foose!

- **Toyota Tundra** The Tundra made Edmunds.com Editors' Most Wanted Vehicles list. It is capable of just about anything. The base model 4x4 is priced around $27,000 and comes with a 4.0-liter DOHC engine that gives out 236 horses. But for those who need big power and can spend more, it has an available 4.7-liter V8 and a 5.7-liter V8 kicking out a hefty 381 horses! The Tundra has unbelievable tow capacity, part time all-wheel drive, and a ton of other special features. It was named Edmunds.com's Most Significant Vehicle for 2007.

- **Porsche Cayenne** With a base MSRP of about $44,000, the Cayenne, which has receieved accolades from Edmunds.com, is sporty and luxurious with an incredible body design. Its 3.6-liter V6 engine delivers a commendable 290 horsepower and gets an average of 20 miles per gallon on the highway. It has full-time four-wheel drive, a solid suspension system, and it comfortably carries five adults. Safety features include stability control and electronic traction control. Everyone I know who owns or has driven this SUV cannot say enough great things about it.

In the past several years we've seen the trend move away from minivans in favor of SUVs, compact SUVs, and wagons. But for those who still find the minivan most practical, here are my top two choices.

- **Honda Odyssey** With a base MSRP of about $26,000, the Odyssey is Consumer Reports' top-rated minivan. It was also one of Edmunds.com's Editors' Most Wanted Vehicles. The

Odyssey has a spacious and luxurious interior, and the engine delivers a solid 244 horses. It is surprisingly agile and handles very well. When driving it, you almost forget it's a minivan! It has a rear-seat DVD entertainment system for the kids, XM satellite radio and an available navigation system with voice recognition. The Touring model comes with a 360-watt audio system. It's loaded with impressive safety features. This is a perfect family vehicle!

- **Toyota Sienna**  The nice-looking Sienna starts at a base MSRP of about $25,000. Toyota's engineers actually did research on families and kids in order to design a minivan that's ideal for families with children and meets many different needs. To occupy the attention of the little ones, there is an available rear-seat DVD entertainment system, while for adults there is an available 10-speaker audio system, touch screen navigation, and Bluetooth and satellite radio capabilities. The 3.5-liter engine gives the minivan some nice power, and safety features include side curtain airbags in all three-rows, side-impact door beams and three-point seatbelts in each seat.

# REDUCING GAS PAINS
# (THE AUTOMOTIVE KIND)

**W**hen my grandpa, Oscar Hansen, was still living, I had a little dispute with him regarding professional athletes and their earnings. He played pro hockey in the 1920s for Chicago, Minneapolis, and St. Louis and was the NHL's leading scorer, back when players hardly made money for the sport. He and his brothers were supposed to represent the United States in the Olympics, but they had complications with their birth certificates. When I told him that Wayne Gretsky and today's pro athletes made millions of dollars in salary and endorsement deals he found that almost impossible to believe. He thought I was surely mistaken. Things were obviously a lot different in his time. If Grandpa were alive today and I told him it costs me more than three dollars a gallon for gas in California, he would think I was somehow mistaken again!

Whether driving a compact car that has a small fuel tank and gets great gas mileage or an SUV with a monster tank and heftier fuel bills, trips to the gas stations these days hurt. With my V8 engine and all of the driving I do, it costs me more than fifty dollars to fill my tank every week. Ouch!

With steep fuel prices setting record highs, everyone I know is trying to find ways to control the costs of driving. Obviously we can't predict whether gas costs will stabilize, climb, or fall. But let's play devil's advocate and assume prices are going to get steeper. The only way to lessen the pain is to try to conserve fuel. Here are some tips to help you save fuel and cash.

## Smaller Is Better Sometimes

The easiest way to get the most drive time for your dollar is to buy a vehicle that gets good gas mileage. Compact cars with smaller engines are the best way to go for those who want to save cash. As you know, I've recommended many cars that fall into this category.

## Consider a Hybrid

Many people are now turning to hybrid vehicles that are powered partly by gas and partly by electricity. Most manufacturers now offer hybrid versions of their most popular cars and SUVs. Hybrids have a bank of high-efficiency batteries that store electrical power. The car's engine is ignited by gas in the combustion chamber, and once it reaches a steady speed, the engine switches over and the vehicle is then driven by the electrical power. Then, when demands on the engine become too high or you want to brake or accelerate, the car starts running on gas again. While the fuel is burning in a hybrid vehicle, the engine puts out more power than necessary, and the excess is stored in the battery banks, accumulating there until the car is ready to drive on electrical power again. Hybrids combine the best traits of a standard engine (some decent power and the ability to drive for many miles without needing to recharge or refuel),

with the best traits of electric vehicles (quiet operation and no pollution).

Relaxing after having removed the engine from Lance Armstrong's GTO.

Electric powered autos are not new to the road, no matter how cutting edge hybrids seem to be today. There was a time in the early 1900s when electric vehicles were quite common. In fact, it was an electric car that set the first land speed record of 39.3 miles an hour back in December of 1898. The following year, an electric car achieved the one mile per minute record for the first time, beating gasoline-powered engines to that milestone handily. In fact, that was during a time when the average gas-powered vehicle went only fifteen miles per hour. Electric cars remained in the market well into the 1930s. But problems with batteries made them less and less competitive with gasoline engines. Battery technology was much less efficient in those days, and batteries were heavy, which affected power and drivability. Electric cars reached a point where piling on more batteries to improve the driving range made the car too heavy to function well. Most of the antique electric cars on the road would only run for about forty miles before they needed to power up again. Even back in those days, that wasn't quite enough mileage to run errands and get back home to recharge the batteries.

With improvements in battery technology, electric cars are starting to look more and more feasible for daily driving, especially with some of the hydrogen technology that's coming out of today's labs. We're now experimenting with hydrogen and other types of fuel cells to power our vehicles that are easier on both the environment and our wallets.

Hybrids are a very hot trend right now and are becoming increasingly popular. I compare driving hybrids to wearing fake fur. I think we will get to a place in the next several years where it will be a faux pas *not* to drive a hybrid.

Toyota was the pioneer in manufacturing hybrid production cars. Its Prius model gets an estimated sixty miles per gallon in city driving, and around fifty miles to the gallon on the highway. That's unbelievable! Unlike standard vehicles, hybrids are at their most efficient in moderate speed city traffic, where they can rely almost entirely on their batteries for propulsion.

With the success of the Prius, the rest of the automotive world jumped into the pool and began developing hybrids of their own in order to remain competitive. Now the Camry, the Lexus RX 400H, the Ford Escape, the Mercury Mariner, and the Honda Insight, Accord, and Civic come in hybrid models, among many others that are just hitting the market or are currently in development.

If you're considering buying a hybrid, check to see what tax breaks are offered with the package. That is yet another benefit of owning a hybrid car. Congress offers tax incentives to buyers in order to encourage the development and sale of hybrid vehicles. These incentives are valid with the first sixty thousand hybrids a company sells, after which the amount of the tax break is gradually reduced as the number of vehicles sold increases. Some states offer matching tax rebates as well. For instance, in California and Colorado, federal and state rebates can cover nearly a quarter of the cost of a new mid-priced hybrid. Most total rebates are more than a thousand dollars and, depending on the model, can run as high as three thousand dollars. There are also government incentives to hybrid ownership, such as access to high occupancy vehicle lanes in many major cities and preferential parking in certain places. Some forward-thinking companies offer additional benefits to their employees for purchasing hybrids, like preferred parking and financial incentives.

This wealth of bonuses certainly makes hybrid vehicles an attractive buy. Of course, the pride of doing the right thing for the planet doesn't hurt either. It's clear why the sales of hybrids are taking off so well. And with the high fuel efficiency and lower gas bills that come from driving one, it's enough to make any car owner smile—especially Al Gore.

## *Making Your Ride More Efficient*

Regardless of the type of vehicle you drive, here are some basic ideas to help your ride perform more efficiently and conserve fuel. Some of these suggestions are pretty elementary, but they will all help keep money in your pocketbook and fewer emissions in the atmosphere.

The first one isn't so easy to follow—I'm still working on it myself! **Drive the speed limit.** When you're zipping along at speeds above 60 miles an hour, the fuel needed for every mile driven starts to increase. For every 5 miles per hour above 60 mph, you generally lose a few miles per gallon in fuel efficiency, depending on the make and model. So screaming down a deserted stretch of highway at 90 mph for many miles at a time could not only get you a citation and a trip to traffic school (not on my list of favorite things to do in the world), but it will decrease your fuel efficiency by as many as 8 miles per gallon. You'll pay at the pump for being a speed demon.

Another trick might take a little of the fun out of driving experience as well (sorry), but it does have its advantages in both safety and fuel savings. **Try not to drive too aggressively.** Peeling out, flooring it at lights and stops, doing burnouts, and tailgating all guzzle gas. Driving moderately could improve your fuel economy by as much as one third.

Another way to cut down on fuel costs is to **drive at steady speeds.** One of my pet peeves is riding with drivers who constantly pump the gas pedal or ride the break. Not only is it nauseating for the passengers, but it wastes gas. It's much more economical to remain at steady speeds. For this reason, whenever you have the opportunity, give your foot a break by putting your vehicle on cruise control.

Another way to save fuel is to **get the junk out of your trunk.** (That phrase just had me singing a familiar Black Eyed Peas tune I love.) Every unnecessary pound you carry while driving robs mileage from your fuel efficiency, as well as possibly becoming a hazard in the event you are rear-ended. Yes, there are certain things you need in your trunk: an emergency kit, jumper cables, tools, etc. But eliminating the things you *don't* need will save you

## What do you think of nitrous? If I want to add horsepower to my ride, is nitrous the best way to go?

Nitrous will definitely add horsepower. But in my opinion, it's really best for racing. I wouldn't recommend nitrous for first-time car owners or those who aren't extremely familiar with how to responsibly use it. In many vehicles, you have to take your hand off the wheel in order to push the nitrous button for extra thrust. At high speeds, that isn't safe. I recommend getting an airbox or supercharger or modifying your exhaust system for added power instead. Save nitrous for the racetrack.

## How can I tell when it's time to buy new windshield wipers?

If the wipers are down to the metal and scraping your windshield, or if the rubber is worn and not properly cleaning the windshield, your wipers need to be replaced. Weather conditions will have a big effect on the life of your wiper blades. In L.A., it very rarely rains. Aside from cleaning bird droppings, smog, and bugs off my windows, I don't often use them. If you live in Seattle, though, chances are you will be replacing your blades much more frequently. New wipers start around fifteen bucks for basic replacements. You can pick up new ones at auto parts stores and gas stations. You might ask an attendant to help you change them the first time. You'll quickly see how easy it is and probably be eager to do it yourself the second time. It takes about two minutes per blade.

## What's the best way to get rid of a funky smell in the car?

First you want to get to the root of the odor. If it is caused by something fairly temporary like wet dog smell or gas fumes, cracking your windows will probably do the trick. If the odor is caused by something that lingers like spilled milk, I suggest getting a detailing job that includes shampooing and/or cleaning the seats and carpets. If you want to be creative and resourceful, try leaving an open container of scented cat litter in the vehicle, spraying a cleaning product like Febreeze on the seats and floors or placing a dryer sheet with a scent you find appealing under the seats.

## What is a chassis? Is there a difference between a chassis and a frame?

Chassis and car frames are synonymous. There is no difference besides the fact that the word chassis sounds fancier.

money. If you have plans to play golf on Sunday, there is no reason to lug the clubs along with you all week to work.

Another simple tip to keep your car fuel efficient is to make sure to **keep up the recommended maintenance for your ride.** A clogged air filter can reduce your gas mileage by more than one third, as can an engine in need of a tune-up. Both factors make the engine have to work harder, which wastes fuel. Under-inflated tires can also knock miles off your fuel economy. And keeping your oil changed can help improve gas mileage by reducing or eliminating friction in your engine. You should be getting tune-ups at least twice a year.

Another suggestion is to try not to turn the vehicle on and off frequently. If you plan to run into your house to grab something you left behind while a buddy waits in the car, or you're waiting outside a convenience store while a friend goes in to quickly grab a snack, it's better for fuel efficiency to leave the vehicle running than to stop and start the engine again. However, don't ever leave the car running while pumping gas or with children inside the vehicle. My mom asked that I share this story: Once when my sister, Jordyn, and I were small children, my mom left us strapped in our car seats with the car running one afternoon while she quickly ran into a store (that was located at the top of a steep drive) to pick up some film. As she walked out of the building, she watched in horror as the vehicle rolled backwards out of the lot, onto the highway, down two hundred feet, and then came to a stop, literally blocking the flow of traffic on a major highway. It's a miracle we weren't hit by oncoming traffic! One moment of convenience could potentially have cost lives. Please don't take chances with your children's safety. However, whenever it's entirely safe and makes sense, leave your car's engine running to conserve fuel.

Also, each time you start your vehicle with a cold engine, you consume more gas than when the engine was already warm. So if you can **take care of five errands in a single trip,** such as while at the shopping mall, as opposed to making five separate trips, it will help beef up your gas mileage.

I do love cruising around in my T-Bird, so it's important for me to follow the tips I've shared with you in order to conserve fuel and protect our precious environment. I hope you will do the same to get the most out of each mile you drive.

# AUTO THEFT AND HOW TO AVOID IT

Before you buy your ride, you might want to consider some basics about auto theft. Did you know that, according to the National Insurance Crime Bureau, roughly $7.6 billion dollars worth of motor vehicles were stolen in 2004? That equates to one vehicle every twenty-six seconds, for a total of more than 1.2 million stolen autos last year. Yep, pretty frightening statistic. Thankfully, mine wasn't one of them. Hopefully yours wasn't either. I know many people who weren't so fortunate. Although any vehicle could be snaked at any time, some models disappear more frequently, and auto theft is definitely something to consider when shopping for your ride. Purchasing a car that is statistically a prime target not only means that it could likely vanish while you're shopping, but it also means you're going to be paying a higher insurance premium to drive it. You can actually save money on premiums by choosing a car or truck with a low theft rate. Insurance companies take these stats into account when determining their rates, which provides a great incentive for the buyer.

According to the Highway Loss Data Institute, the Cadillac Escalade was number one on the list of most commonly stolen vehicles in the United States last year. The Escalade is definitely a hot and desired ride. For every thousand Escalades on the road, 13.2 were stolen. One out of every hundred was stolen in 2005. Most thieves wanted the entire SUV, while some stole them for the parts. The vehicle's flashy wheels are the most targeted item. Because of these statistics, Cadillac installed a much better anti-theft system in their 2007 models, which includes an ignition immobilizer. My sister Jordyn drives an Escalade, so I imagine she looks forward to incorporating this new technology into her ride.

On the flip side, the least commonly stolen vehicle is the Ford Taurus, which has a theft rate of 0.3 out of a thousand, or slightly less than one in every three thousand. There is a monster difference in odds there, which makes it understandable why certain vehicles come with hefty insurance rates.

The Lancer Evolution is the second most commonly stolen ride in the States, also due to the car's fancy wheels and rear spoiler. Vehicles with attractive wheels and flashy features make for common targets for car thieves. Thieves are also drawn to Xenon headlights, a cool feature that put the Nissan Maxima and Lexus RX 330 at the top of the stolen car list as well. Nissan is retaliating by pioneering a program that involves spraying microdots with unique identifying numbers on certain parts of these cars. The identifying numbers are impossible to remove and make every stolen part traceable.

Other tasty targets for thieves are Dodge Rams and the Ford F-250 and F-350. The Honda Civic, Toyota Camry, and Honda Accord are also perennials on the list, because with popular models like these the parts are interchangeable. There is great profit to be made in dismantling and selling parts.

I'm not suggesting you don't buy one of the cars or trucks that are on the top stolen list. I'm just urging you to think about the risks before you buy and look into anti-theft technology to combat it. Thankfully the auto manufacturers are constantly inventing technology to deal with this issue so we can continue driving the cars and trucks we love!

## Keeping Your Ride Safe from Sticky Fingers

I recommend following what is referred to as the "layered approach," which means trying several different methods simultaneously to prevent your ride from being stolen. No one thing is likely to stop a determined car thief, but many different strategies combined at once will probably deter them.

The simplest and most important thing to remember is to always lock your ride, and don't ever leave a spare key in the vehicle. Even if you feel you're in a safe area, lock up. It's also a good idea to park in well-lit areas and close to where you are going to be so you can keep a look out for trouble, or at least listen for your car's alarm. If you don't have a car alarm, I recommend getting one installed. Although alarms are frequently triggered accidentally and often people don't pay attention to them, they may scare off a thief who is new to the game, and you will likely notice your own alarm if you hear it. Every bit of protection helps.

If you can afford it, I recommend installing some kind of tracking and transmitting device in your car. Prices are coming down on these devices, and they are extremely effective. GM's OnStar system comes standard with many of their models, along with a year's subscription to its various services. OnStar tracks your vehicle at all times, so it will inform GM service centers of where you are in the event of an emergency, and it will locate your vehicle if it is stolen.

LoJack is similar in function to OnStar's tracking device. It functions as a hidden transmitter that allows police to trace the location of a vehicle equipped with the system. It can be purchased as an add-on for most vehicles. LoJack has a better than 90 percent success rate in returning stolen vehicles to their owners. I recently heard a story about a man who bought LoJack for his sports car. The car disappeared, and he called LoJack to find it. They immediately tracked its precise location—it was found at the end of a pier on the bottom of the ocean!

Many auto thieves will steal a vehicle and immediately drive it into a semi-truck or packed flatbed to avoid being spotted by police. OnStar and LoJack will find these cars regardless of the fact that they are hidden from view. Another benefit to using tracking systems is that most insurance companies offer discounts to owners who equip their vehicles with these "passive anti-theft devices."

The only cases when OnStar and LoJack won't help is when the owner of the vehicle discovers that it was stolen too late and the car has already been delivered to a chop shop. Chop shops are where vehicles are taken to be stripped down for their parts. By that point, the LoJack system has likely been separated from the vehicle.

Another excellent crime deterrent is Powerlock, which is effective against hotwiring. This is roughly the same system that Cadillac is adding to their 2007 Escalade. It's available as an aftermarket add-on. Since nine out of ten car thefts involve hotwiring (that tenth stolen car is put on a tow truck to be moved), the system can be really useful in preventing your car from being snaked.

The system works by installing an interrupter in a sealed casing in the ignition system. The owner of the Powerlock-equipped vehicle is given a coded key that overrides the interrupter, allowing the car to function normally. But if the vehicle is running without that coded key, it shuts down after forty-five seconds and simply won't start again until the appropriate coded key is used. The code keys are impossible to clone, and the system will continue to work even if the battery and electrical system is taken out or disrupted. The system is about as tamperproof as anything on the market, and it comes with a lifetime guarantee. Powerlock costs only a few hundred dollars with the installation fee, so if you live in an area where auto theft is a problem, it's definitely worth considering.

The old steering wheel immobilizers can be useful against amateur thieves, but they aren't likely to deter the professionals. Pros pour liquid nitrogen over them and then shatter them with a quick tap while the metal is super-cooled. Or they saw through the steering wheel, which isn't nearly as tough as the immobilizer. It only takes a few seconds for a savvy car thief to remove the device from the wheel. On the other hand, steering wheel immobilizers are inexpensive and easy to use, and several auto manufacturers offer significant payments if your vehicle was stolen while the device was properly installed on the steering wheel. If you read the fine print and use the device correctly, the cash from that guarantee will generally cover your insurance deductible if your ride is swiped.

Kill switches on the ignition are also inexpensive (they cost as little as ten bucks), easy to install, and they work well. However, they don't prevent a thief from hot wiring.

Another useful and inexpensive theft deterrent is a steering column protector. Because a thief has to crack open the steering column to hot-wire the vehicle, hardening it can keep your ride from being targeted in the first place. Both permanent and temporary models are available as aftermarket add-ons.

I recommend checking with local law enforcement officials to see what kinds of trouble your neighborhood has with auto theft. Then purchase anti-theft protection according to your needs and what is affordable. Driving a tricked-out T-Bird with fancy Foose wheels in Los Angeles makes me a prime target. Therefore, I'm cautious: I always lock my car, I park close to where I'll be shopping or in meetings, I have a car alarm, and I'm planning on purchasing LoJack. Please be careful so that your ride remains in your hands.

## What does it mean when I apply the brake pedal and hear a strange noise?

A squeaking sound when you apply the brakes typically means the pads are low or you're low on brake fluid. If your brakes are making ANY abnormal noises, have them checked immediately. You don't want to take any chances with your brakes, as you could be damaging parts of the brake system that are costly to replace, or they could begin to fail while driving. *Note:* When driving through puddles or wet areas your brake pads will get wet. Be aware that your brakes won't function as well as they will under normal conditions. But they will dry quickly when back on dry ground.

## What's the best way to ensure that my wheels won't get stolen?

Wheel locks can be purchased at most high-end specialty shops or wheel specialty shops and some auto stores. They function by locking one keyed lug nut on each wheel. Somebody recently attempted to steal my wheels and ended up with nothing but the center cap. Because I had the keyed lug nuts, the thieves got a little Foose swash, and I kept my four wheels.

## Is it bad to run the gas tank to nearly empty?

It's not a good idea. First of all, there is a greater chance of water and sediment getting into your fuel lines and engine. Also, a low fuel level increases gas vapors in your tank, which may create the spark for a fire. It's pretty unlikely you would start a fire, but you never know! It's best to keep your gas tank at least half full at all times, especially during winter months in freezing climates.

## Do burnouts and 360s hurt the life of my tires?

Yes, of course they do. They're fun, and I admit I've done them! But both burnouts and 360s are very hard on both your tires and drivetrain, which will wear out more frequently, costing you in the long run. Not to mention, you risk the possibility of getting slapped with a citation for being reckless on the road.

## How often do I need to change my spark plugs?

Mechanics will most likely include a spark plug check during a tune-up. Be sure to ask if this is included as part of the service. And always request the old spark plugs back so you know they actually replaced them. If you notice backfiring or sputtering in your engine while driving, it's a good idea to take your vehicle to a mechanic and have your plugs checked immediately.

# YOU FOUND YOUR RIDE!

**C**ongratulations, you've chosen your ride! After doing all of that thorough researching, test driving, and inspecting, I hope it's exactly what you wanted and is the ideal car or truck for your lifestyle. I imagine you look very cool behind the wheel!

Buying or leasing a vehicle is like having a new best friend. You're now committed to that ride for the long-term, or at the very least for the *short* long-term. For better or worse, until the lease is up or you find a new buyer, it's yours. Hopefully you are excited about that and end up loving your ride and giving it a cool name. Every month when you make that payment or recall the purchase price, it'll remind you that, in some ways, it owns *you* as much as you own *it*. After the energy and money spent searching for and purchasing the perfect ride, I assume you want to preserve it the best you can. Rather than have a cavalier attitude about caring for your car or truck, I encourage you to take pride in it and remember that it's an extension of you. The fact that you're reading this book is a fantastic start.

Proper car maintenance will not only spare you stress and costly repair bills

down the road, it will make your vehicle last longer, look nicer, run better, use fuel more efficiently, hold its resale value, and cause less pollution. And it'll keep you and everyone else safer on the road. You'll also *look* better because the way you care for your ride is a reflection of you. Wouldn't you say it's worth it?

Your vehicle is comprised of systems, the components that make up those systems, and features. Systems are the series of components that actually make your car go, and features are the things that make it comfortable and attractive, like bucket seats, leather interior, or dubs. If you've ever been to a stock-car race, you know that you don't need many features to have a working vehicle. But then, you wouldn't want to drive a stripped shell with a metal bench seat back and forth to the office either.

Taking care of your car's features is almost as important as taking care of its systems to ensure that you and your vehicle have a long and happy relationship. Both the systems and the features can benefit from a proper break-in period.

In later chapters, we'll discuss the systems in some detail, but for now, let's just take a look at what we're dealing with. The major systems in your vehicle are:

1. The powertrain—the engine, transmission, axles and driveshaft
2. Lubrication/oil
3. Ignition
4. Filters
5. Electrical
6. Emissions/exhaust
7. Fuel
8. Brakes
9. Tires
10. HVAC (Heating, Ventilating, and Air Conditioning)
11. Cooling
12. Belts
13. On-board computer

## Breaking the Systems In

New vehicles have new systems, and new systems have new components. Makes sense, right? Well, often previously owned cars have new components as well. And, just like on anything mechanical, new components benefit from a break-in period. The process of breaking in a vehicle means driving it so that the systems are exer-

Filthy from working on a Monte Carlo during *Overhaulin'*.

cised and parts can wear into each other slowly and properly. This will help extend vehicle life.

Breaking in your ride is like running a marathon. It's best to start at a slow, even pace before transitioning into a full run. In vehicular terms, this means avoiding heavy loads on the powertrain for the first two hundred miles. The powertrain is comprised of all the parts of the engine that connect the transmission with the drive axle(s) of your car. Starting at full-throttle, towing trailers, and packing the vehicle with heavy loads place extra force on all the moving parts in the drivetrain and should not be done right away. Although you might assume the new components in the powertrain are ready and capable, extreme exertion within those first couple hundred miles is not advisable.

As you drive your car or truck, oil lubricates the moving parts, preventing unnecessary rubbing and damaging of components and allowing everything to function smoothly and seamlessly. But

### Is it worth trying to refurbish an engine, or is it better to just buy a new one?

That's largely a question of time and economics. It depends on the magnitude of work involved. Years ago, it was cheaper to have an engine rebuilt than to simply replace it with a new one. Now, however, labor costs are higher, and you may find it's less expensive to purchase a new engine. The new engine or crate motor will also come with a warranty, while the rebuilt engine may not. That's a huge bonus.

### How do I know the maximum weight that my vehicle can withstand?

Rule of thumb: One passenger per seatbelt. If there is the same number of passengers as there are seats and belts in the vehicle, you are fine. Cars have what's called a gross vehicle weight (GVW) and a curb weight. The curb weight is how much the vehicle weighs when empty. The GVW is the maximum safety performance weight. You should never exceed your manufacturer's recommended GVW.

### I hate the way my front license plate looks on the car. What can I do about that?

I hear you on this one! I feel the front plate on a car takes away from its aesthetic. In California we're required to have front plates, but it mars the beautiful body design. I believe the manufacturers feel this way too, and that's why so many sports cars don't have a place to easily mount a front license plate. After receiving a ticket for driving without my front plate, I reluctantly put it back on in a creative way, without drilling holes for the bracket. Feel free to be creative with your brackets and application, while being good and obeying the laws for your state.

### My boyfriend wants a new exhaust system. What are the advantages and how much should he spend?

After-market exhaust systems look cool, sound killer, and will increase horsepower and torque. The systems have fancy mufflers and tailpipes that either mask sound or create that deep rumbling, throaty effect. It's a lot like music—some like classical, while others prefer rap. A big exhaust company will tailor the system to fit your individual preferences.

pushing the engine too hard too soon puts unnecessary stress on the powertrain and forces the uneven surfaces together. This causes wear. Wear is the number one reason for auto repair, and it can and *will* cost you dearly. Proper break-in allows the components to polish down gradually, maximizing powertrain performance and minimizing premature wear. I know you might be eager to get in your brand new ride and punch it to see what it can do, but trust me, that isn't a good idea, at least right away. After the initial couple hundred miles you've driven at moderate speeds, and without loading all your friends into the back seat or pulling a trailer, the vehicle's components will be properly broken in and ready for normal operation. And at that time you can feel free to step on it and test that baby out! However, there are exceptions to this rule. In certain high-performance vehicles, putting the pedal to the metal right away may be acceptable or even encouraged. Consult your owner's manual or ask your dealer to be sure.

The secret during the break-in period is to do everything moderately. Drive your ride the way your driver's ed instructor taught you. Well, maybe don't be *that* extremely cautious and slow! But try to go easy and keep the engine's rpms (revolutions per minute) in the bottom half of the rpm range. On many engines, this is below about 3000 rpms. Occasional three-quarter throttle acceleration is okay, as the increased gas pressure in the combustion chamber helps the rings to seal.

If your car has a manual transmission, be aware of proper shift ranges. Always change gears when the rpms are too high or too low for the gear you are in. Driving in too high a gear at low speeds makes the engine work harder, or "lug," and driving in too low a gear at high speeds also makes it work harder and could ultimately blow your engine.

Our grandparents' cars needed to be driven at low speeds for *several* hundred miles in order to properly break in the components. This is no longer the case, even with new engines and crate motors. Superior manufacturing and engineering have made the break-in process much shorter. Depending on how far the dealership or seller is from your home (my T-Bird came from a dealership in another county), it's possible that you will have broken in your new ride or engine by the time you turn into your driveway. A few hundred miles of obeying speed limits and traffic flow is more than sufficient.

If your vehicle was previously owned, this process is not necessary. The break-in period is long over and you can step on it, test that baby to the max, and move straight on to maintenance.

# EARLY MAINTENANCE

Once your ride is broken in, your maintenance begins. The first step to proper car care, you might be relieved to know, doesn't involve a grease rag and a lug wrench. All you need is paper and a pen. Setting up a maintenance log, while definitely not as exhilarating as driving your new ride, is just as important.

Several systems in your vehicle require frequent routine maintenance. These include the lubrication system, the filters, the tires, and the belts. Other systems require periodic maintenance, and you'll benefit from studying your owner's manual carefully to fully understand when and how each system should be checked for safety and functionality.

As you go through your owner's manual, set up the pages of your maintenance log. You should have a page dedicated to each system. Put the date you purchased your vehicle and the current mileage as the first entry on each section of the log. Since most maintenance recommendations are based on mileage, you can't predict ahead of time exactly when you'll need to have your systems inspected, but you can estimate pretty well based on your driving trends. I suggest having tune-ups at least twice a year or at every 3,000 or 4,000 miles, and more frequently if you're hard on your ride. Unless you drive your vehicle very infrequently, you will almost always reach the recommended mileage mark before your date mark. I do every time. So it's extremely important to keep a record of when maintenance was performed on your ride and what the odometer read at the time in order to ensure you are performing maintenance at the proper intervals. Standard entries in your log should include:

1. Oil and oil filter changes
2. Other lubricant changes (brake fluid, power steering fluid, transmission fluid, etc.)
3. Air filter changes
4. Belt checks
5. Tire rotations
6. HVAC (heating, ventilating, and air conditioning) checks
7. Emissions checks
8. Any other recommended maintenance by your vehicle's manufacturer.

While you're creating your maintenance log, you might also want to take the time to set up a fuel log as well. First, this information is helpful during tax time. Did you know you can deduct the distance you commute to and from work in most professions and the miles driven for any charitable endeavors? (Despite this tip, *The Garage Girl's Guide to Everything You Need to Know About Taxes* will not be hitting bookstore shelves anytime soon! And of course you should check with your tax professional before claiming a deduction you aren't sure about.) A log will also help you track gas mileage over periods of time and allow you to detect any patterns of change early on. Drastic fluctuations in fuel consumption indicate potential engine problems. In those cases you'll want to see a mechanic right away. Additionally, a fuel log will let you know how efficiently your vehicle performs and will allow you to better track costs and expenses. Stow the book in your glove compartment in order to stay organized and so that you'll always have it on hand to refer to and update when necessary.

## Gas Mileage Log

One simple way to document and track your car's gas mileage is to use a gas credit card. Your monthly statement will list not only the amount owed but the gallons consumed and the price per gallon. You can then check your mileage gauge for the miles driven and use the number of gallons consumed figure to compute your gas mileage during that billing period. You can review the statement when it comes in the mail or check it out online.

If you don't have a gas card, there are two kinds of fuel mileage logs you can keep. The first one is the most important to your vehicle's operation. It should include the date, the number of gallons purchased, the odometer reading, the distance traveled since your last fill-up (odometer reading minus the last reading), the miles per gallon, (number of miles traveled divided by the gallons of fuel purchased in your last fill-up), and whether any additives were mixed into the fuel.

Many auto manufacturers recommend using a fuel additive (like STP gas treatment or, in the winter, HEET or Iso-HEET) once a month when filling the gas tank. These additives work by drying out the fuel tank, engine, and related systems, therefore keeping rust and corrosion to a minimum. They also prevent water from entering the fuel hoses. Water in the gas mixture could make your car's engine skip or freeze, causing a fuel blockage in cold weather, making it tough or impossible to start your vehicle.

Water finds its way into the fuel through condensation on the top of the gas tank when the tank has a lot of air space and also during a fill-up when water droplets get into the fuel. This generally happens when a gas station is low on gasoline in its source tank. The way to avoid getting polluted gas would be to know when a station receives its fuel supply. The best time to fill your tank is the day after the fuel supply arrives, when water and pollutants have had time to settle to the bottom. If you see a truck delivering gas to the station, I suggest you keep on driving.

A standard gasoline log should look like this:

| Date | Odometer Reading | Miles Traveled | Gallons Purchased | Miles per Gallon | Fuel Additives |
|------|------------------|----------------|-------------------|------------------|----------------|
|      |                  |                |                   |                  |                |
|      |                  |                |                   |                  |                |
|      |                  |                |                   |                  |                |

I've included a full-page version of this log in the Appendix so you can create your own. If you want a homemade version, you might also consider buying a notebook, using thumb-tabs to separate the sections, and creating a log that way as well.

The second type of gasoline log, which is also in the Appendix, is the kind from which you need to deduct miles traveled for work or charity from your income taxes. I have deducted many miles this way for both business and philanthropy, and it definitely adds up in the end.

As I mentioned before, if you notice any strange fluctuations in your gas mileage, be sure to take your vehicle to a mechanic as soon as possible, and show him or her (I love when it's a her!) the gas log. It's likely there is a problem, and it will benefit you to detect it early on.

## Service Log

It's important to keep a service log that includes everything that's been done to your ride. This serves a number of purposes. It will increase your vehicle's resale value because the prospective buyer will see that the car has been properly maintained and repaired. It will make it easier to diagnose any problems that may stem from a previous repair. And it will help keep any warranties in effect during the life of the vehicle.

Below is a sample of a typical maintenance and service log, which I strongly urge you to maintain.

| Date/Mileage | Location | Service Performed | Parts Replaced | Observations and Warranty Information |
|---|---|---|---|---|
| 10/9/2007 46,295 miles | Joe's Autobody, Sepulvida Blvd, LA | Oil change, fluid check, filter check | Oil, (10/30 weight) oil filter, air filter | Change oil again at 49,295 miles or 1/9/2008, whichever comes first; inspect air filter at 51,295 miles |
| | | | | |
| | | | | |

Again, I've included a full-page blank version of this log in the Appendix. I recommend checking your fluid levels and tire pressure regularly. There are many advantages to this, which I will outline in detail in later chapters.

## Interior Maintenance

If you're like me, there were certain features that drew you to a particular car or truck. Body style, performance stats, interior design, and the paint job are just a few of the things that make vehicles unique and personal to us. Just as your ride's systems need proper care if you want them to last, so do these features. For maintenance of specialty features refer to your owner's manual for any specific instructions. I've listed some basics here to get you started.

If your vehicle has a leather or vinyl interior, it's important to purchase a quality leather or vinyl conditioner from your dealer or an auto parts store and follow the instructions on how to carefully treat all the seats and surfaces. Over time, exposure to heat and sun can cause drying and cracking. Our family learned this the hard way while driving convertibles with leather and vinyl interiors in Florida. The seats and dashes cracked badly over time. My mom and dad urged us to properly care for the leather and vinyl in our cars. It takes very little effort and saves a lot of money in the long run. Also, it's essential to read the labels carefully when purchasing conditioning products, as not all products are approved for both vinyl and leather surfaces.

The top of a vehicle's dash is especially prone to cracking because it takes abuse from direct sunlight. A friend of mine has a twenty-five-year-old Volvo, and the dashboard crumbled in her hand while she was driving along the freeway. A little protection on that dash—applying a conditioner every few months—would have made a tremendous difference in preserving the dashboard's surface.

It's also a good idea to purchase a folding sun shield to cover your dashboard during daylight hours. This not only prevents heat from building in the interior, but also shades and protects your surfaces. I recommend buying one for the back window as well. You may think it cramps your style a little bit, but trust me, it is worth it.

For cloth seats, you should treat the fabric with a good stain protector. These are available in the automotive section or home-care product section of most local discount stores. Look for a product that's approved for both upholstery and carpet, and follow the directions carefully. Don't forget to spray your floor mats and carpeting at the same time you clean the seats. Try to do this on a warm day when you can leave the car doors open for an hour

Changing the oil on my T-Bird.

or so to let the product cure. A simple dose of fabric protector will pay huge dividends on muddy days or in the event something spills on them.

Treat your tires and wheels with protective lubricants and polishes to keep them strong, healthy, and shiny. This will prolong their life and keep them looking beautiful!

# EMERGENCY GEAR

**I**n this chapter I'm going to outline for you the emergency essentials that I believe you should have in your ride at all times. If you don't have an onboard satellite communication system like On-Star, it's a good idea to have a cell phone and cell phone charger in the vehicle with you so that in the event of an emergency you will be able to call for help. This is especially important if your car has been giving you trouble, if it's late at night, or if you're driving long distances.

Pretty much all vehicles come equipped with a jack and lug wrench specifically designed for changing the tires on that particular car. They are usually located near the spare tire, either under a carpet that flips up inside the trunk or underneath the trunk lid. Many cars and trucks also come with small toolboxes. My mini toolbox, jack, and lug wrench are all located under a carpet flap with the spare tire in my trunk.

An additional item you might consider keeping in your trunk with the tire changing tools is a three-foot piece of steel pipe large enough to fit over the han-

Not your standard
emergency!

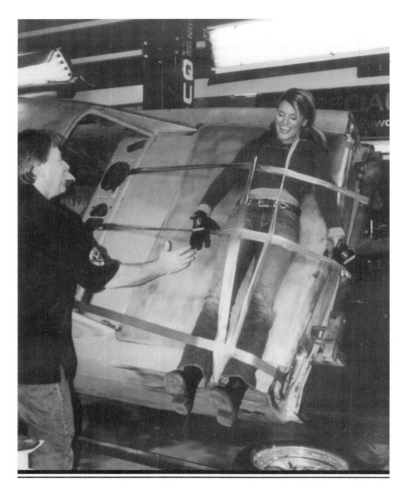

dle of your lug wrench. This pipe can be helpful in many situations. First, the added leverage can help you remove even the
most stubborn lug nuts. In service centers and garages, technicians use pneumatic, or power, wrenches to loosen and tighten
lugs. Over-tightening is common, and unless you are very strong,
getting lugs off in the event of a flat tire without a pneumatic
wrench might prove difficult. Sliding the pipe over the lug wrench
provides extra leverage, and even the most stubborn lug will
likely pop loose.

Another advantage of the steel pipe is that it can make the process of raising the vehicle with the jack less tedious and work intensive. If you use the pipe to extend the pumping handle of your jack, you accomplish the lift without having to bend as far and stress your back to do the job.

And lastly, in the event of a frustrating car ride, the pipe can be used to quiet that annoying backseat driver. Just kidding . . .

Here is a list of items I recommend carrying in your vehicle at all times. To remain organized and keep them dry and clean, store them in a plastic bin:

1. First aid kit
2. Jumper cables
3. Can of Fix-a-Flat

Doesn't perform like the T-Bird . . . but a fun ride to cruise around in on set!

4. Bottle of fresh drinking water
5. Some kind of prepackaged snack such as dried fruits and nuts
6. Flares with lighting instructions
7. Emergency fold-out triangles for road-side emergencies
8. A flashlight with separate batteries (don't store the batteries in the flashlight where they can corrode)
9. Work gloves and/or vinyl disposable gloves
10. Basic tool set—screwdrivers, crescent wrenches, small hammer, and pliers
11. Can of WD40
12. A few rags (at least one white one for use as a signal in an emergency)
13. Hand sanitizer—I use it to clean my hands after each gas fill-up
14. Extra washer fluid
15. Thermal or small blanket
16. Extra cash
17. Pack of matches or a lighter

If you *really* want to be thorough and prepared for any situation, the following are additional items that I believe are also important to have in your trunk. They will take some extra room, but you'll be glad you have them if you need them.

18. Small fire extinguisher rated for all kinds of fires
19. Four metal wheel chocks for blocking tires or, if you want to be resourceful, four pieces of 2x4 wood about six inches long
20. A box of baking soda (good for odors, fires, and cleaning battery cables)

21. A small jar of petroleum jelly
22. An old toothbrush (great for cleaning batteries and engine parts)
23. Fifty-foot length of 3,000-pound test nylon or jute rope—useful for towing
24. Gallon of coolant or water (for radiator leaks)
25. Quart of motor oil
26. Empty gas can
27. A disposable camera to take pictures at the scene of an accident, should one occur (having a camera in my car was a great benefit to me in two different accidents)

For winter driving in snow country I suggest always having the following:

28. De-icer
29. Snow/ice scraper
30. Portable snow shovel
31. Winter gloves
32. Ten-pound bag of sand or kitty litter for traction
33. Snow chains (if you live in an area where snowstorms may occur)

In the glove box, make sure to keep the following:

1. Your owner's manual
2. Maintenance log book
3. Registration and insurance information
4. Contact numbers for family members, roadside service, the local police, fire department, and ambulance
5. Tire gauge

### My convertible top is filthy. How do I clean it cheaply?

Pretty basic. Use a commercial vinyl or leather cleaner designed for autos, and follow the directions on the bottle.

### I have dogs. Sometimes I take them out to the woods or to the beach. What are tips for protecting my car while they're dirty and traveling with me?

Most auto accessory stores, pet stores, and online sites sell seat covers and floor mats specifically designed for this purpose. If your vehicle is large enough, the best and safest plan is to transport your dog in a kennel. This will save your upholstery and keep your pet safe. Allowing pets to run loose in your ride could potentially cause an accident. While traveling down the freeway, my sister's dog, Esther, once sprang forward and managed to put her Escalade in neutral. If it isn't possible to travel with a kennel in your ride, lay a protective mat or blanket on the seats, and be sure to properly restrain your dog. Pet stores now sell seat belt adapters for pets and booster seats (for smaller dogs) so that they can sit safely and comfortably and still see out of the windows. Cute!

### What's your opinion about hybrid cars? Do they really make a difference? What are your thoughts?

I think we're moving in an important direction. Fortunately, hybrids and electric cars are getting hipper every day. The auto manufacturers are making them bigger, more powerful, and more stylish to appeal to consumer desires. Now we even have hybrid SUVs. Hybrid vehicles make a huge difference in protecting our air and environment. They are more economical because of lower fuel consumption. There are so many choices I'm having a hard time deciding which one to get!

### Is it true that I should turn the air conditioning off in order to conserve fuel?

Yes. Cooling the passenger compartment requires more effort from the HVAC system, which puts more stress on the engine. More work for the engine means greater fuel consumption. However, another opinion is that lowering your windows instead of running the AC interferes with the vehicle's aerodynamics, which also consumes fuel. I feel it's still better to kill the AC.

### Is it true that I should turn off the radio if the vehicle is low on gas?

No. The radio's power comes from the battery, which is electrical. The battery is kept alive by the alternator. If you're low on gas, drive slower and crank the tunes!

6. Pencil or pen

7. Small flashlight (check batteries regularly, or get the kind of flashlight that you crank or shake so that it can be used without batteries)

8. Can of pepper spray or mace (check local restriction to make sure carrying it is legal, and also make sure the can is operable and not outdated)

9. Personal medical information that emergency technicians may need to know. You might not be conscious at the scene of an accident, and emergency personnel will need to know about any special medical needs you have. You might also include your blood type, the name and phone number of your physician, any specialists you consult, and who to contact in the event of a major emergency.

One item that I keep in my garage that I think is genius and I really get a lot of use out of is a "Power Board" or "Hot Shots" case. It's a small, portable, lightweight case with cables for jumping a car and an air pump for filling tires. You plug it into an outlet to charge it and it comes in very handy. I got mine at an auto parts store for $60. They're also sold at big box stores and home improvement stores like Home Depot. The air pump can also be used for filling beach balls, innertubes, soccer balls, and air mattresses. It's a worthwhile investment that I highly recommend.

# BASIC TOOLS

Although you might not ever plan to pick up a tool other than your lug wrench (I hope you'll at least attempt to use that!), you never know when a tool might come in handy and provide a quick fix on your ride. I believe it pays to have an understanding of the basic tools that are found in most sets.

Personally, I love working with tools. Power cutters and sanders and plasma cutters are a few of my favorites. Those are slightly harder to operate and call for some instruction and an air compressor. But there are many tools commonly used day to day that are small and simple to work with. I urge you all to read about the tools in this chapter so that, at the very least, you'll know what to grab when someone asks you to find the ratchet and $3/8$-inch socket.

Professional mechanics use professional, quality tools supplied by mobile tool companies, such as Matco Tools. For the rest of us, auto parts stores and big box department stores carry a large selection of tools for the simplest to most involved auto repair. You can also find the basics at many gas stations, although I don't recommend purchasing them there unless you need them in a pinch. And just like

Combination wrenches.

with your other shopping needs, the Internet is a terrific place to buy tools as well. I like Matco the best and have lately been going directly to their Web site when I need something.

### Wrenches

Wrenches are the most common tool used in auto mechanics, which is why engine work is often referred to as "wrenching." If you want to use the vernacular and sound like a pro, ask a friend if they want to go "wrench on your ride." This tip is especially good if you want to get out of doing some of the work yourself!

Wrenches come in both *standard* (or SAE) and *metric* measurements. Check your owner's manual to see what kind of measurement system your vehicle uses. It might use a combination of both.

Socket wrench.

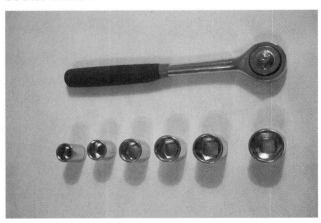

There are many types of wrenches. Some of the most common are open-end, close-end, combination, Allen wrenches, and the oil filter wrench.

Combination wrenches are great because they have the open-end style on one side and the box-end on the other. I have a combination wrench set for both standard and metric measurements with wrenches of various sizes. It was an inexpensive purchase and has been extremely useful to have on hand.

Socket wrenches are both standard and metric and normally come in sets of varying sizes. The sockets have square holes in the center that fit over a square on a tool with a long handle, known as a ratchet. There are also different size ratchets, although you normally need only a small one and a large one. I have a socket wrench set that is metric on one side and standard on the other because my car uses nuts and bolts of both measurements. The set cost me less than $15.

Allen wrenches.

Combination wrenches, sockets, and ratchets are used all over the car and within the engine compartment. But you would most commonly use them for loosening the oil drain plug and changing spark plugs.

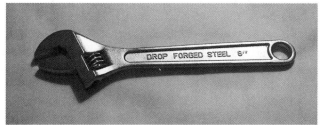

Adjustable wrench.

Allen wrenches are shaped like an L, have a hexagon-shaped head, and are used for fitting into small, unique holes. Like all tools, Allen wrenches come in various lengths and sizes. They are

The two different kinds of oil filter wrenches. I prefer the one on the right, but both do the job.

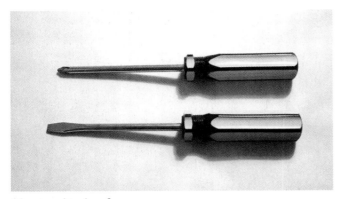

The two kinds of screwdriver, Phillips *(top)* and regular *(bottom)*.

not quite as common as other wrenches, but a set is very inexpensive.

Adjustable wrenches are often referred to as "monkey wrenches." By turning the wheel on the head of the wrench you can adjust the head to fit around nuts and bolts of different sizes.

There are two main styles of oil filter wrenches. One has a strip of metal shaped in a circle that fits over the oil filter and is supported by a handle. The other type is the one I prefer. It's about two inches deep, looks like the top of a thick can and has grooves inside to grip the oil filter as you turn it.

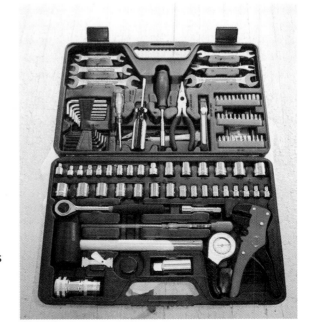

A well-stocked tool kit is essential to being prepared for every eventuality.

## Screwdrivers

There are two types of screw-drivers: standard and Phillips. As you probably already know from doing home repairs, the standard screwdriver has a thin, flat head and is used for turning screws that have one thin slot. The Phillips screwdriver has a rounder, sharper head with four little points that is used for turning screws with an "X" design on them.

You never want to use the wrong screwdriver with the wrong screw because you could damage the screw or hurt yourself.

Grinding in the engine compartment of a Mustang at SEMA.

Screwdrivers come in various lengths and sizes. The size needed for the job depends on the size of the screw, the space you have to work with, and the leverage needed to loosen or tighten the screw. They are most commonly used for tightening screws in the interior, dashboard, and headlight and taillight assemblies, as well as for fastening covers in the engine compartment, such as the air filter cover. Screwdrivers are also vodka and orange juice. So if you're of age and you're finished driving for the day, you might consider mixing yourself one and moving on to the next chapter!

# PARTICULARS OF THE POWERTRAIN

Since I was a little girl, I have been fascinated by engines. The way they sound, their complexity, their ability to make vehicles run, their power, and of course their speed! During time spent at racetracks and in garages throughout my life I've observed and studied quite a bit about engines. And most recently, I've had the honor to work with and learn from some of the greatest mechanics in the world through my work on *Overhaulin'* and *Powerblock*. Now, unless you plan to be a mechanic yourself one day, it's not essential that you know every intricate detail of engine operation. But I do believe it's beneficial and exciting to understand the basics about that awesome block of power that makes your wheels turn. If you know a little bit about what makes your car tick, it can really add to your love and appreciation for your ride.

While a lot of this book delves further into the information and tips that allow you to be more hands-on with your ride, this chapter will give you a fundamental overview of your engine and its components. Isn't it amazing to think about the pioneers of the automotive world who took us from horse and buggy to the auto-

An internal combustion engine.

mobile and then to ponder how far we have come since the early 1900s? The first Model T engines put out about 20 horsepower. Today, top fuel dragsters boast roughly 8,000 horsepower and travel at speeds over 300 mph. Wow . . . Henry Ford would be proud.

Engines are complex systems. While most of us are comfortable checking tire pressure and washing windows, engines are pretty enigmatic and can be slightly intimidating. Poking at hoses and changing spark plugs definitely call for mechanical skill.

That nervousness you may encounter around your vehicle's engine is understandable. Even if at one time you learned to tweak a carburetor with a screwdriver and listen for the change in its purr, the same techniques no longer apply in modern cars and trucks, because now we operate mostly with electronic ignition systems. Engines are ever developing. Although they're now more complicated than in the past, they've also become more fuel efficient and longer lasting. These are all positive factors, but it means that a lot of the simple mechanical techniques the novice could once handle now must be left to the pros.

The engine is a powerhouse, the heart and soul of the vehicle.

My goal is to help you better understand how your engine operates and hopefully become more confident with all things under your hood. So let's take a look at what makes those wheels turn.

## Carburetors vs. Fuel Injection Systems

Most modern cars and trucks have electronic ignition systems, which are computerized systems that control and time the release of electrical currents and the fuel/air mixture into the engine to make it run. Older vehicles and the classics we love have carburetors. Though these are two very different methods for mixing fuel and oxygen to operate an engine, the outcome is the same. At the heart of every functioning engine, controlled explosions take place hundreds or thousands of times per minute and make your car's wheels turn.

My friend Kevin Byrd from Ford Racing gave me a great explanation during one *Overhaulin'* build a couple of years ago. Here is my translation of Kevin's analogy: Like a woman is an enigmatic species, a fuel injection system is an intricate and complicated computer. No matter how much you analyze it and attempt to understand it, you can never fully comprehend its complexity.

A carbureted engine—the carbureetor is fitted on top.

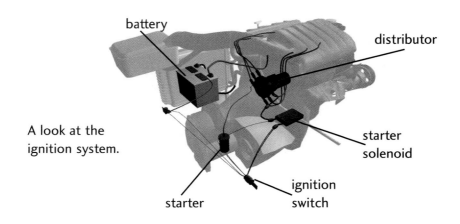

(We women will take that as a compliment, Kevin!) In general terms, a fuel injection system is a computer that controls the amount of fuel and air that is mixed in each engine cylinder prior to combustion. These systems are found in all modern vehicles.

Carburetors are the small, square metal boxes located on top of the engine underneath the air filter. They are simpler, non-computerized devices that mix fuel and air before running it into your engine. You will see carburetors on most older vehicles and muscle cars.

Cutaway view of a car's engine and transmission in a front-wheel drive vehicle.

## How the Engine Ignites and Moves the Car

When you turn a key in the ignition, electrical power is converted into a high-voltage spark that is carried to a starter solenoid. That solenoid accumulates power and ignites the starter motor. The starter motor then powers the flywheel, which starts the crankshaft turning, which puts the engine's pistons into motion. While

A look at the ignition system.

battery

distributor

starter solenoid

ignition switch

starter

this happens, gasoline makes its way from the fuel tank through the fuel lines to the combustion chamber, where it's mixed with air and forced into the cylinders.

The number of cylinders determines the size and power of an engine. I drive a V8 (or eight-cylinder engine) that puts out roughly 350 horsepower. A four-cylinder ride would offer significantly less horsepower, and a V12 could boast upwards of 500 horsepower. Pistons fit into the cylinders (one in each), allowing just enough room for the fuel and gas mixture to enter. The spark plugs sit above the cylinders. They receive charges or sparks by way of the wiring system and the vehicle's battery. As the fuel/air mixture is pushed upward in the cylinders by way of the pistons, the sparks meet the fuel air mixture and create explosions. The pressure from the explosion forces the pistons back down again. As the pistons continue to move up and down, the rods at the top of them do as well. Their movement also keeps the crankshaft turning. The pressure of the piston rods is transferred to a crankshaft, which moves the flywheel faster. The flywheel is attached to the transmission, which allows the power to make its way there. A great force has been created, and once the car is in gear, the wheels begin turning, and the vehicle is set in motion!

Cutaway view of the inside of a piston.

As the engine runs, it continuously pumps oil and fluids through the car's systems, making the transfer of energy possible and cooling and lubricating the engine's many moving parts.

## Engine Displacement

The total space in the cylinder when each piston is fully extended is referred to as engine displacement. The more volume there is for fuel to fill the cylinders, the more powerful the engine is. Because only a certain amount of fuel/air mixture can fill a given volume, the available room in the cylinders is the limiting factor to how much power can be pulled out of that engine. If a cylinder is overloaded with too much fuel for the space, the excess gas is left unburned and expelled. These days, in the interest of fuel efficiency, there's a system in most engines in which any unburned gas left behind after combustion occurs is recycled back into the engine and reused. This helps cars run much cleaner than they did in the past.

Because engine displacement is an important factor for determining power, it is generally noted in a vehicle's description. In order to keep a standard measurement among engines throughout Europe and the United States, that volume is given in liters. My T-Bird has a 3.9-liter engine.

## *Understanding the Alternator*

As an engine runs and the crankshaft turns, a belt at one end of the crankshaft transfers the engine's energy to the alternator. The alternator uses the mechanical rotation from the engine to create

A close-up look at an engine without the valve covers.

electricity. It then transferrs that energy to the battery to recharge it as the car runs, enabling it to power things like the radio, headlights, clock, ignition system, and power locks.

## *Engine Blocks*

An engine block is a beautiful "block" of metal with holes drilled into it designed to perfectly accept the metal pistons that are the powerhouses of the engine. Many blocks are made from cast iron, an iron alloy that resists corrosion. Other blocks are made from cast aluminum to cut down on weight and help improve fuel efficiency. Both types have advantages. Cast iron can rust and weighs about three times as much as aluminum, but it's also very durable. Aluminum is a lot lighter and won't corrode, but it's not quite as strong. Regardless of what the block is made of, today most pistons are made from aluminum. The lightweight metal helps cut

A look at the inside of an engine block.

down the amount of fuel it takes to set the pistons in motion by two thirds, helping the engine perform more efficiently.

In the search for ways to further reduce engine weight and improve gas mileage, I've heard that engine designers are experimenting with high-tech plastics for engine blocks. However, I haven't yet seen any of the prototypes. Until then, my heart still belongs to the big cast-iron beauties.

A beautiful new engine with the valve covers on. Notice the belts up front.

## Big Blocks vs. Small Blocks

Big block engines have bigger bores (holes) and larger combustion chambers, which equal more horsepower and torque and, consequently, more fuel consumption. Small blocks can be bored out for larger fuel displacement, which adds power. A big block or a bored out small block is the better choice when you're going for power. If economy is more important and your vehicle isn't typically going to be pulling or transporting a lot of weight, small blocks make more sense. Remember that superchargers and performance intake systems can be added to both big blocks and small blocks to create additional power relatively inexpensively. Love that!

## Engine Types

At one time, just about every car on the road had the same kind of engine. But then, nearly all cars were identical. Henry Ford used to joke about his Model T, "You can have it in any color you want, as long as it's black." Things have broadened in our modern age of personal choice and diversification, and now there are many different types and sizes of engines. There are four-, six-, eight-, and even twelve-cylinder engines. Some take gasoline, gasohol, or diesel fuel, while others are electric-powered or a hybrid combination. The basic differences have to do with engine power and fuel consumption. Generally, the more power an engine has, the more fuel it burns. Vehicles with heavy tow capacities need more powerful engines that can withstand the stress of pulling massive things like trailers or boats. Compact, lightweight vehicles can utilize smaller engines with less power in order to maximize fuel economy. The number of cylinders an engine has directly equates to its power. V8s (eight cylinders arranged four to a side in a V shape inside the block of the engine) are found in SUVs, full-size pickups, racecars, and full-size passenger vehicles. Compact economy cars usually have four-cylinder engines. Since the difference in gas mileage and initial price can be substantial, it's important to make sure you know what you want to drive and how you plan to use your vehicle before you buy it (see chapter 1, Finding Your Ride).

### Superchargers

Superchargers are systems that can be connected to the fuel injection system to create more power than the cylinders provide in an engine. They work by forcing a greater amount of air into the gas mixture, which increases the engine's horsepower and torque. They are a perfect way to get more power out of a smaller engine without having to upgrade to a bigger size, which weighs and costs more. Weight is a big factor in all cars and helps determine how the engine performs. Lighter cars burn less gas and perform more efficiently. Supercharging is a way to keep weight down but still increase power. All Indy cars are supercharged. Many, if not most, street racers are supercharged as well. NASCAR doesn't allow superchargers because they prefer stock engines and actually aim to restrict power and keep all drivers on a level playing field.

Superchargers come stock in many production vehicles. They can also be purchased and added later to most cars, trucks, and SUVs, as long as they make hood clearance. If you want to put more muscle under the hood of your ride, a supercharger is one great way to do it.

## *Even Simpler Than Turning a Key*

The days of getting into a vehicle and turning the key are nearly gone. Manufacturers are now designing rides that are equipped with high-tech remote ignition systems. Similar in design to garage door openers, remote starters work by sending a radio signal to a component within the engine, "telling" it to start. Generally, remote starter devices contain a button on the keychain that enables you to start the car from a distance or while the key is in your purse or pocket. Remote starters are great for extreme climates where you don't want to experience the initial discomfort resulting from those pain-in-the-butt waits in the car while the engine runs and either cools or warms the passenger compartment. With the remote, you can have the climate controls pre-set accordingly and ignite the engine while inside a building, enabling you to slide into

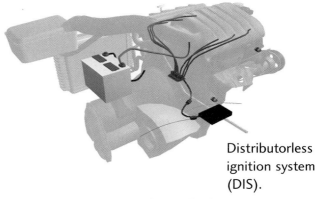

Distributorless ignition system (DIS).

the driver's seat in comfort. These systems are available from dealerships as an option on certain vehicles, and they are a common and reasonably priced aftermarket add-on. Remember the days before we had TV remotes and had to get up and *walk* to the set to change the channel? Now we don't even have to twist our wrist to start our cars. You have to love technology!

I don't know about you, but little excites me more than talking about engines and horsepower! I hope this overview helped give you a better understanding of engine basics and how the moving parts work together to propel your ride.

## *Transmissions*

On a rear-wheel drive vehicle, the transmission is located behind the engine on the rear side between the engine and the driveshaft.

In a front-wheel drive vehicle, the transmission fits either at the back of the engine above the driveshaft or to one side of a transverse-mounted engine.

There are two types of transmissions: automatic and manual. When driving a vehicle with an automatic transmission, you don't need to worry about switching gears. The transmission will automatically shift gears as you accelerate and decelerate, remaining within the ideal RPM range and allowing the engine to perform at its best. A vehicle with a manual transmission has to be operated by the driver using a foot clutch to disengage the gears and a gear-shifter to switch them in order to travel at different speeds and keep the car within the ideal RPM range. Manual transmissions are considered more fun for driving high-performance sports cars because they allow the driver to dictate when the car shifts into a higher or lower gear, thereby giving the driver more control over the power output and speed at the various RPM ranges. An automatic transmission is obviously less labor intensive and is great for drivers who spend a lot of time in traffic. Vehicles with manual transmissions are generally less expensive. I prefer driving manual transmissions over automatics, but because of the amount of time I spend in traffic, my daily driver is an automatic. If you don't know how to drive a manual transmission, I highly suggest you learn. Not only is it fun, but you never know when it will benefit you to know how. You might unexpectedly be a designated driver one evening, and the vehicle you need to drive home is a manual five-speed. Or you might have the opportunity to test drive some killer sports car with a manual transmission. You wouldn't want to miss out on that!

Regardless of whether your ride has an automatic or a manual transmission, the function is the same. The transmission takes the revolutions per minute from the crankshaft and transforms that

Transmission.

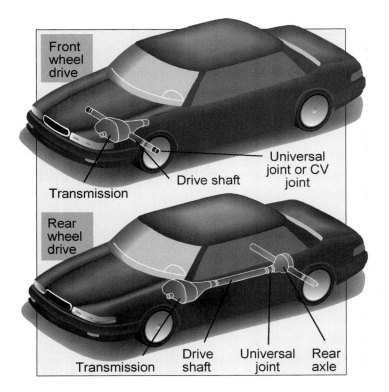

On a front-wheel drive vehicle, the transmission is generally located to the side of the engine and below it.

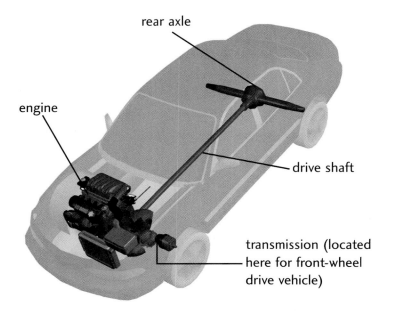

rear axle

engine

drive shaft

transmission (located here for front-wheel drive vehicle)

steady mechanical energy into a varied number of speeds. If your engine's power was transferred directly to the wheels without first going through the transmission, it would mean your car would only be able to operate at one speed. The transmission gives your engine its range of speeds.

# SUMMARY OF YOUR SYSTEMS

**Y**our car operates by way of a variety of systems. Each one is important, and together they keep your car running right. This chapter will give you an overview of the systems in your vehicle.

## The Electrical System

Today's cars and trucks have many electrical systems that are interwoven and complex and are responsible for powering things like your radio, lights, clock, automatic seat adjusters, and seat warmers. Each of these systems must have a steady and continuous source of energy. Standard components in the electrical system include the battery, the battery terminals, battery cables, the starter, and the alternator/generator.

## The Emissions/Exhaust System

Emissions systems first appeared on cars in the 1960s when consumers and manufacturers began to realize the potentially devastating effects of fossil fuel emissions

An electrical system.

Battery.

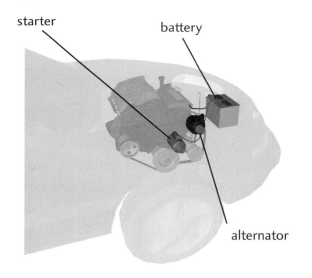

starter

battery

alternator

The alternator.

on the environment. If your new vehicle was manufactured prior to 1960, your emission system probably consists of only a muffler and a fuel tank. Post 1960, however, new government standards brought new requirements for pollution control. On today's sophisticated vehicles, emission systems still contain a muffler and

The emissions system.

a fuel tank, but they now have a catalytic converter, an air injection pump, a vapor canister, and various sensors and solenoids that reduce emissions rates to acceptable standards. If you live in certain parts of the country, like California, regular smog emissions checks are required.

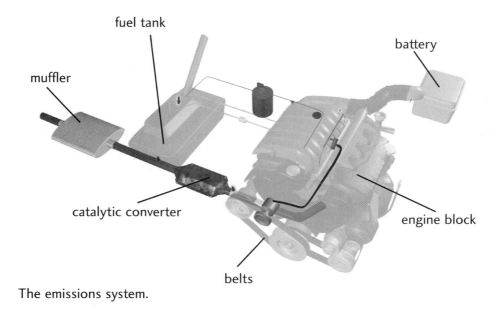

The emissions system.

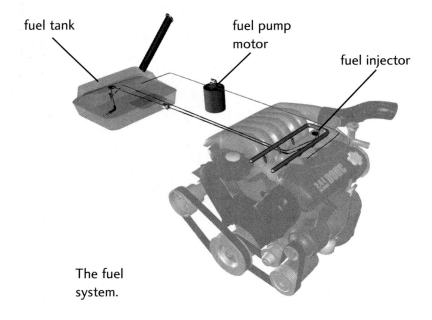

fuel tank

fuel pump
motor

fuel injector

The fuel
system.

## The Fuel System

The fuel system is closely tied to the emissions system. The fuel system delivers and stores, by way of electronic control, the precise amount of fuel into the cylinders of the internal combustion chamber. Today's vehicles also monitor fuel vapor losses that can occur due to cracked filter lines, vapor hoses, and loose gas caps. The basic components of the fuel system are the fuel tank, the fuel pump motor, the fuel pump, the fuel pressure regulator, the fuel injector, and the fuel filter.

## The Brake System

In technical jargon, the brake system is a complex network of components that are hydraulically powered, providing the necessary friction to stop your vehicle's wheels. In simple terms, that means that the brake system on your car is a fluid-driven system. When you press on your brake pedal, the pressure goes from the master cylinder in the engine compartment, through the brake lines, and ends at the wheels. The master cylinder contains a piston that pressurizes the brake lines, which run from the front of the vehicle to the wheels. The fluid in the lines forces the brake pads to press against the turning rotors, or discs. The friction between the pads and the wheels forces the wheels to stop turning. If you've ever noticed a red or black dust in and around your wheels when you wash your car, you've seen the result of that friction. Over time, the pads grind down as they

Front disk brakes.

press against the rotors. Some vehicles have an alert system built in that warns you the pads are low by creating a shrieking sound or by illuminating a warning signal on the dashboard's instrument panel.

Rear drum brakes.

Putting the rotors and calipers on Lance Armstrong's GTO.

Please don't allow the pads to get that low before replacing them!

In modern vehicles, there are also electronic components that prevent wheel lock-up during hard breaking. These are antilock brakes and traction control or slip differential. In my car, the ABS system won't even allow me to do a good peel-out unless I deactivate it first. However, I sure do appreciate the ABS system kicking in when I have to make a sudden stop or when I'm driving on slick surfaces.

There are two different kinds of brake pad systems: disc brakes and drum brakes. Most modern vehicles have disc brakes. Some still have drums in the back. The disc brakes are more efficient and are used in the front because they are the workhorses of the system. Essentially the difference, besides the parts involved, is that drum brakes have less friction on the surface than disc brakes and don't withstand high heat conditions as well. Drum brakes tend to wear down much more quickly than disc brakes and require more maintenance. All modern vehicles are built with break systems that are more than adequate to stop the wheels, even when the engine is running at peak speeds. You also have an emergency brake (or E-brake, also referred to as the parking brake), which works independently of the braking system. The emergency brake is manually operated in order to provide breaking power in the event of hydraulic failure.

Disc brakes.                                    Drum brakes.

In old movies when the hero is racing down the side of the mountain having discovered that the villain has clipped his brake lines, if he would simply apply his emergency brake, he could have avoided the inevitable tire-squealing, knuckle-whitening descent at 100 mph. Of course, then the movie wouldn't have been nearly as exciting. You and I would rather live, so please remember the emergency brake in the event that your brake system fails.

Stunt drivers also use the E-brake for tricky driving maneuvers when they need a vehicle to spin in a controlled manner. But please *don't* try this at home because it's absolutely terrible for your car.

## Heating, Ventilating, and Air Conditioning System

The HVAC system is the comfort control center of your car. A small heater core and fan produce and direct heat from the hot engine into the passenger compartment of the vehicle. All modern cars have a heater and most now have air conditioning systems as

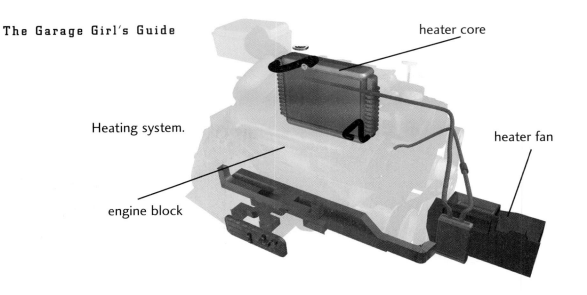

heater core

Heating system.

heater fan

engine block

well. Air conditioning is produced by a belt-driven compressor that uses Freon to dry and cool the air before it enters the passenger compartment. The HVAC system keeps you comfy while driving your ride.

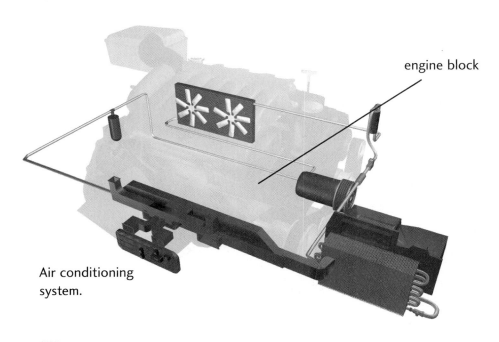

engine block

Air conditioning system.

## Engine Cooling System/Radiator

Your radiator is the only safeguard against your engine overheating and potentially failing. It utilizes water, coolant (or radiator fluid), and air to keep your engine cool. On hot days it keeps your engine from over-heating, and in the wintertime it utilizes anti-freeze to keep the fluids in your engine from freezing.

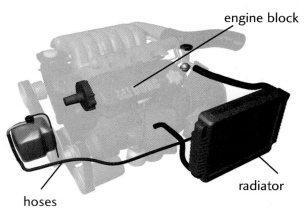

Engine cooling system.

## Lubrication System

Your car runs with the help of many lubricants and fluids. Every moving part on your vehicle is protected and/or powered by some type of fluid or grease. Later in the book, I'll cover what each of these fluids is, where to find them, how to test them, and when to top them off.

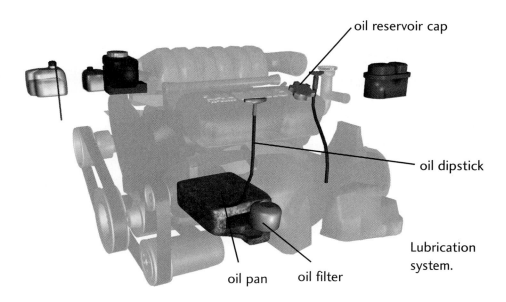

Lubrication system.

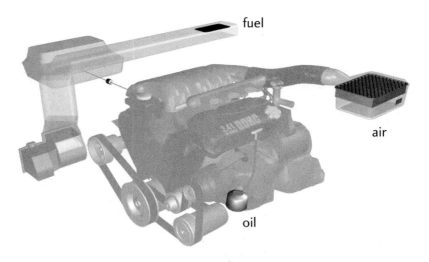

fuel

air

oil

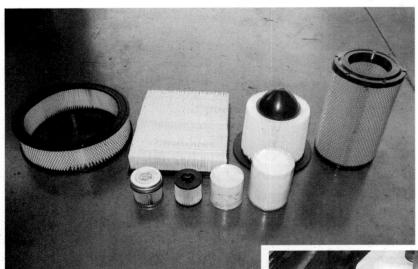

Filters.

Air filter.

## Filters

Filters ensure delivery of uncontaminated fluids and air to your engine. Regular maintenance is essential for proper performance and long vehicle life. Your car has an oil filter, an air filter, a crank case filter, a fuel filter, and possibly a cabin air filter. Oil filters should be changed every time your oil is changed. Air filters should be changed once a year or every twelve thousand miles, and if you live in an area where there is a lot of pollution, or the desert where there is a lot of sand in the air, you should change the air filter more frequently. My air filter lasted about a year in L.A., and when it looked clogged and filthy recently, I replaced it myself quickly and easily. Your dealership service center or mechanic should let you know if and when all filters in your vehicle need to be replaced. Keeping them properly maintained will really impact your engine's life and performance.

## Belts and Hoses

Belts for components like the fan, generator, and water pump are connected to pullies and are critical to proper engine operation. Hoses, like the radiator hose, carry fluids throughout your engine to keep the components functioning and lubricated. Your vehicle has two kinds of belts: a timing belt and accessory belts. The timing belt ensures that vital engine components are properly aligned. Accessory belts operate major system components like power steering, the water pump, the crankshaft, the alternator, and the A/C compressor. The belts used by the different components and systems vary among vehicle makes and models. Your engine's belts and hoses should be inspected during tune-ups and replaced as needed.

As I hope you are beginning to see, modern cars are incredibly complex and phenomenal pieces of machinery. We're so used to

seeing them and using them every day that we often take them for granted. Airplanes and spacecrafts are thought to be so incredible, I think largely because we don't have experience with them on a daily basis. But automobiles are just as fascinating, maybe even more so because we get to control and operate them ourselves—and choose which one we like best. America fell in love with the automobile back in the 1930s, and it's been a love affair ever since!

# DO-IT-YOURSELF MAINTENANCE

**W**hether you drive a Charger with a HEMI, a full-size pickup with a V8, a compact car with a buzzing four-cylinder, or a hybrid vehicle, the key to your ride's long life and, consequently, to your own satisfaction, is proper maintenance and upkeep. Maintenance is all about keeping the systems of your ride running and functioning properly so that your vehicle will last longer, keep you safer, and save you money.

You might want to copy the part of your owner's manual that deals with scheduled maintenance and keep it handy in your log, checking off the recommended services as you do them. Documenting everything will keep you organized, and being diligent about servicing your ride will help your vehicle last longer, drive better, and retain its value. I also recommend keeping a file of maintenance receipts. This will be great should you decide to sell your ride. That upkeep log and the corresponding service receipts will show the potential buyer that you were conscientious with the car or truck during the time you owned it. This will give the buyer more confidence in the vehicle and hopefully get you a higher dollar in the sale.

In the case of emergencies, and when talking with mechanics, it's advantageous to know your vehicle and its maintenance schedule inside and out.

In addition to frequent oil changes, you should have a full tune-up at a service station or your dealership at least twice a year to ensure all systems are being properly serviced. Although you will periodically take your vehicle in for service, it's easy to conduct a lot of the maintenance checks yourself, and I'm going to walk you through each system of the vehicle and tell you how you can do most of these routine checks on your own.

Maintenance goes beyond an oil change every three months. Certain tasks, like checking tire pressure, should be done weekly. I suggest walking around your vehicle and taking a look at it every couple of days. Airplane pilots do this before every flight. It takes just a minute or two. Are the tires low on air? Do there appear to be any foreign objects lodged in the tread? What about the windshield wipers? Are they properly affixed? Are there any cracks or holes in the headlight or taillight covers? Are there any leaks underneath the car?

As part of this check, I also suggest turning the lights and blinkers on once a week and walking around the vehicle to make sure they are functioning properly. It's the best way to ensure that no bulbs are burned out or are burning more dimly than their counterparts. It only costs a few dollars to replace a brake light bulb. It could cost a few thousand to deal with the damage to your car if the bulb burns out and somebody rear-ends you or if the police catch you with a missing taillight and slap you with a citation. In these cases you're also looking at an inflated insurance premium.

I realized the other day that my left taillight had burned out, so I took my T-bird to an auto parts store, picked up the lightbulb I needed, grabbed my tool kit from my emergency stash in the trunk, and changed the bulb right there in the parking lot. Yes, I had to remove the whole taillight assembly to change it, but it took less than ten minutes, cost me under five dollars, and it was gratifying!

These are all simple maintenance tasks that too many of us often overlook in our haste to jump behind the wheel and get where we're going.

Beyond the basic maintenance tasks, there are additional routine checks. Two main factors will determine your maintenance schedule: time and mileage. Some systems or parts of your vehicle will require maintenance regardless of whether you drive the car or truck very often. For instance, motor oil. Motor oil will break down over time, building up viscosity and becoming dark and sludge-like. Even if your car just sits in your driveway or you drive very few miles, the oil still needs to be changed every three months in order for the engine to run properly.

Brakes, on the other hand, will not wear down as quickly, unless you spend a lot of time in stop-and-go traffic or driving in hilly terrain. I'm normally in either congested traffic or the hills of California, which are both very hard on my brake system. I have to replace my brake pads more frequently than the average driver.

When driving down hills, we ride the brakes in order to keep our speed under control, and that obviously wears out the brake pads. With a manual transmission or the Tiptronic that is offered in newer vehicles, we're able to downshift to alleviate the pressure on the brakes, saving on brake wear and tear. Have you ever noticed how cab drivers will often put their cars in park or neutral at stop signs rather than apply the brakes? It's a smart way to make the brakes last longer.

As part of the maintenance check for your brake system, ask your service department mechanics to check the pads, rotors, and hydraulic fluid. And if you ever feel there is a problem with the brakes, immediately take your car in to be looked at. Brake failure while driving could be extremely dangerous.

### Fluids

Plan to check the fluid levels in your car during every third gas fill-up. Some fluids, like windshield washer fluid, require just a quick visual check. The reservoir is either full or it's not. Other fluids require a dipstick check.

### Oil

We already talked about the importance of changing the oil after the first two thousand miles and every three months or three thousand miles thereafter. The exception to this would be vehicles that are being driven under high-performance/high-pressure conditions for extended periods of time. If you race, drive in mountains, do a lot of off-roading, or spend hours a day in traffic like me, you'll need to change your oil more frequently. An oil change is quick and inexpensive, and it is the single most important thing you can do to keep your ride running well .

What type of oil should you use? Your owner's manual will tell you the manufacturer's recommended weight and type of oil for your vehicle. But this is assuming you're driving under normal conditions. If you think you're demanding more of your vehicle than normal, you probably want an oil of a heavier grade. Check with your mechanic or an auto parts store rep to be sure. Also, if you drive in geographic regions where temperatures vary drastically, you will need a different type of oil for winter than you're using during the summer. This may also be true if your driving patterns change throughout the year. Additionally, many additives are available that can increase the protective lubrication of your engine, and these can be especially useful in your oil if your car is old or if you're really putting high demands on it.

The many types of vehicles and engines and the different climates and various driving styles have led to a plethora of choices in motor oils, and it's easy to get overwhelmed. Take a walk down the oil row at your local auto supply store, and you'll quickly see what I mean. Many brands offer oils of various weights and mixes, so be sure to follow your manual or ask a mechanic for the best choice. In the chapter on fluids, I'll discuss this in greater depth and also talk about synthetic oils.

Checking the oil on my T-Bird.

## Checking Your Oil

Checking the oil is a fast, simple job I know you all can tackle. The engine should always be turned off when checking the oil. And for the most accurate reading it should have been cooled for at least ten minutes so that the oil is resting in the pan. If oil is still in the hot engine you may get a false reading, overfill the level, and possibly do damage to your engine.

1. You can use your bare hands for this like I do, or put on your

disposable gloves. Grab a clean paper towel or rag. The rag should be clean so that no dust particles or dirt get into the oil reservoir.

2. Locate the oil dipstick on the engine. It has a ring for your finger at the top and is normally located near the center of the engine. Pull out the dipstick and wipe it clean with the rag.

3. Carefully reinsert the dipstick into the tiny reservoir hole completely.

4. Pull it out and check the level. The end of the oil line should fall somewhere within the "min" and "max" markings indicated on the dipstick. The oil level should not exceed the "max" or "full" mark. Too much oil is detrimental to your engine. If the oil level is lower than the "min" mark, you will need to add some. However, you shouldn't have to add much if you are changing your oil as often as recommended. If you have to add oil on a regular basis, either there is a leak somewhere in the system or your car is burning oil. Both problems should be addressed immediately. By checking your oil every few times you fill your car with gas, you will be able to detect these problems early on. If the oil is dirty (clean oil should be yellow, orange, or clear in color), sludgy, or smells like gas, it's time for an oil change.

5. To add oil, locate the oil filler cap on the engine. It's easy to find and will normally have an oil can icon on it. If you can't find it, consult your owner's manual. Open the filler cap, and slowly add some oil using a funnel or really good aim, being careful not to overfill.

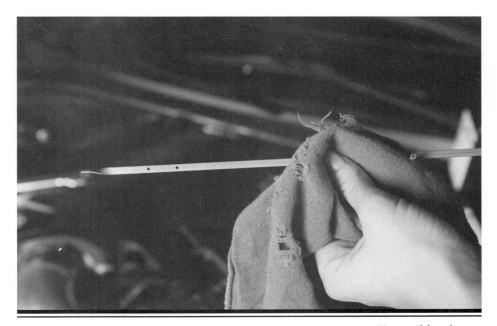

## Changing Your Own Oil

I'm going to walk you through the process, and I have complete confidence that you all can do it! It should take you less than thirty minutes, it'll cost approximately fifteen dollars, and it's gratifying. I demonstrated an oil change on the *Tyra Banks Show* in September 2006, and the young woman I taught changed her oil like a pro on the first try.

Your oil level should be between the min and max (or full) markings on the dipstick.

What you'll need for the job:

- Socket set (Mine has both standard and metric sockets and only cost about $10. Find out what your vehicle needs.)
- Combination wrench
- New oil filter
- Oil filter wrench or high-grade sand paper
- Funnel

- Basin for draining the old oil (I recommend the one with the spout attached)
- Empty container with a lid for transporting the old oil
- Baggie with a zipper or tie for the old filter
- Rags—a clean rag for checking the oil
- Gloves—if you must; I think using bare hands is better!
- Four to six quarts of whatever oil your vehicle recommends (all four-cylinder engines take four quarts of oil, and six-cylinder and eight-cylinder engines take five or even six quarts; your owner's manual should indicate how much oil your engine takes)
- Newspapers or a blanket to sit on
- Something to tie back your hair if it is long; it isn't fun to get oil in your hair

Here are the steps:

Having gathered the essentials, I'm ready to change my oil.

1. Put on some clothes you don't mind getting dirty, drive your car to level ground where you won't be disturbed, and lay out your newspapers or blanket and all your tools.

2. Turn the vehicle off and make sure it's in park with the emergency brake on. Let the engine cool for at least ten minutes. Both the oil and metal will be *very* hot after the car has been running. Also, letting the engine cool will allow the oil to drain from the engine to the oil pan.

3. Gauge how easy it is to slide underneath the front of your ride. If it's difficult to get underneath your car for the job, use your jack to raise the car on one side, making sure to put the jack in the recommended place for your vehicle. Then secure your car on jack stands to be sure it won't fall on you.

4. Put on your gloves if you want to wear them. Locate the oil drain plug nut on the oil pan. It is usually the lowest plug to the ground and may even be labeled. Make sure it isn't the transmission fluid plug. Grab the basin for catching the oil and slide it directly under the oil pan plug.

5. Find the right socket to fit over the nut, stick the socket on the socket wrench, turn the nut counterclockwise, and loosen the oil plug a little bit. If this wrench doesn't work, try the other.

6. Back out of the way, keeping your face shielded from the flow of oil. Remove the plug, and allow the oil to drain completely. It should take several minutes.

7. Locate the oil filter (it looks like a soda can and is typically on the side or back of the engine block) and grab the oil filter wrench. Insert the wrench into the ratchet, put the wrench around the filter and turn it counter clockwise. It shouldn't be that tough to loosen. You may not even need the wrench. If you don't have an oil filter wrench and the fil-

ter is slippery or too tight, a great tip I learned is to grip the filter with high-grade sand paper. It should turn easily every time. Be careful, the filter may be hot, and never allow your face to get too close to it. Pour the oil from the filter into the basin, and set the filter aside.

8. Pop the hood, locate the oil filler cap on the engine (look for the picture of an oil can), and remove it.

9. Grab the new oil filter, dip your finger in the new oil and coat the top of the filter with oil to prime it. This helps it seal better. Put the new filter in place and tighten it by hand. You don't want to make it super tight because you could crush the filter. Your oil filter should be changed every time you change your oil. If you pay to have your oil changed, a filter change is always included. I recommend asking for the old filter back from the attendant so you know it was actually replaced.

10. Put the oil drain plug back, making sure the washer is still there between the nut and the pan. A washer has the same diameter as the nut and fits between the nut and bolt to provide a buffer in order to keep the nut from damaging what it's being tightened against.

11. Use the funnel to pour the new quarts of oil into the oil filler reservoir.

12. After all of the oil has been poured, check the dipstick to see the oil level. The oil level should meet or come close to the word "max" or "full" on the dipstick. Be careful not to fill beyond that point, as it could damage the engine.

13. Start the engine, and let it idle for several minutes. Look underneath the vehicle for any leaks. Check the oil level on the dipstick once more. If everything looks good, you're almost finished.

14. Pour the old oil into the container and seal it. Put the old filter in the baggie. Clean everything around the car, and wash your hands well.

15. Take the old oil and filter to a recycling center, gas station, or oil change center immediately. It needs to be disposed of properly, as it is hazardous waste.

16. Congratulate yourself on a job well done and money saved. You rock!

Underneath the car, locating the oil drain plug.

### *Transmission Fluid*

Transmission fluid is another dipstick check, though you don't have to conduct it more than once a month unless you suspect a problem. Many modern cars don't have a transmission fluid reservoir dipstick. My T-Bird does not. If you have one, locate the dipstick (it's usually near the back of the engine compartment). Checking transmission fluid is a lot like checking the oil. Pull out the dipstick, wipe it down with a clean rag, put it back in, and pull it out again to check the levels. Checking the dipstick fequently will allow you to monitor whether or not your car is leaking transmission fluid. As long as your levels remain stable, transmission fluid should last for years for the average driver.

### *Power Steering Fluid*

This is the cheapest component of your power-steering system. Changing it on schedule helps prolong the life of other, more expensive power-steering components like the power-steering pump and the very costly power-steering rack. Checking the level of the power steering fluid is easy. There is no dipstick. Pop the top off the reservoir (it will be marked with a steering wheel icon), and look inside. If the reservoir is full, the level is correct. If you notice that the fluid level is low, or if you have to add fluid more than twice a year, I'd have the system checked. Other signs that the power steering fluid is low are if it's difficult to steer the wheel, if there's a whiny or groaning noise when you turn the wheel, or if there are leaks under the power steering fluid reservoir. All situations could lead to more serious failure down the road and should be taken care of right away.

Recently, my power steering was giving me a stiff response and groaning every time I turned the steering wheel. I checked the fluid level and realized it was a hair low. So I consulted my owner's manual to find out the recommended power steering fluid for my car and stopped at the local auto parts store to purchase some. I then added a little fluid to top off the reservoir. I felt proud to have tackled the issue myself. However, I quickly realized that the groan hadn't disappeared. I called my

Power steering fluid reservoir.

dad for advice, and he mentioned that the pressure in my tires could be low, causing both the noise and the steering difficulty. As usual, Dad was right. I added some air to the tires, and the problem was solved. (You'll learn a lot more about tire pressure in the chapter on tires.) Please note that recommendations for how often to change power steering fluid vary widely, so you should rely on your mechanic and/or your owner's manual for the proper schedule.

## *Coolant*

Coolant is one fluid you have to monitor regularly, especially when coping with temperature extremes. Keep the system topped with the kind of fluid recommended in your owner's manual. Look at the label of the coolant. Some already come premixed with water so you'll just add coolant straight to the reservoir, while others need to be added with an equal mix of water (I use distilled water). You definitely want to be sure you have the right mix of fluids in your system.

In addition to adding coolant when necessary, you'll also need to completely replace your coolant occasionally. This involves draining your vehicle's cooling system and then replacing the old with a fresh mixture. This is beneficial because the old mix may contain dirt and other particles that could clog the system and cause the car to overheat. Coolants also contain rust-inhibitors to keep your radiator from rusting and seizing up. Water and metal don't mix. Over time, these rust-inhibitors in your system will break down, causing corrosion and rust to accumulate inside your radiator and within your engine block. Repairing that kind of damage can be extremely costly. So it's worth it to maintain a clean and carefully balanced coolant system!

If you live in a geographic area where the temperatures routinely dip below freezing, it's a good idea to get your mechanic to check the concentration level of your coolant every year before the winter months. Coolant that is diluted or weak can freeze when temperatures drop. And if your coolant freezes, your car will overheat, never mind that it's 20 below outside.

Checking coolant levels is very simple. Always conduct the check when the engine is cold. The container is transparent, and there's a "max" line on it to indicate optimum coolant levels. The level in the reservoir should be right at or just below the "max" line. I recommend that you have your cooling system checked at every oil change, and I suggest checking it once before summer and again before winter. Complete fluid changes should occur at 60,000 miles for systems with standard coolant and 100,000 miles for systems with "long-life" coolant. You can find out which you have by reviewing your owner's manual.

## Brake Fluid

Maintaining the proper brake fluid level ensures proper performance of your brake system. A visual check of the clear reservoir to ensure optimum fluid level is generally all you need to do. Your mechanic will check the whole brake system when you service your vehicle. Brake fluid seldom, if ever, needs to be flushed and changed unless your brake system has undergone a major failure.

Brake fluid reservoir.

## Windshield Washer Fluid

You can check the windshield washer fluid by looking in the clear reservoir marked with a wiper icon. Most wiper fluid is blue or clear, so look for the transparent plastic reservoir filled with blue or clear fluid. If the level is low, purchase some washer fluid and fill the container. You don't need a funnel, just do your best to aim well. In the winter, if you live in a place with freezing temperatures, it's important to keep this reservoir full of wiper fluid that is resistant to freezing and to carry a spare jug of it in your trunk. Blown ice crystals and snow can gunk

Windshield wiper fluid reservoir.

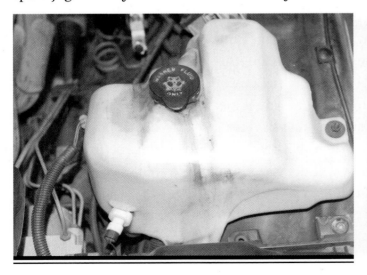

up your windshield and freeze against it. If you don't have freeze-resistant wiper fluid, squirting liquid on your windshield just adds to the frozen mess. I found this out the hard way, having lived through many brutal Minnesota winters. One winter I found myself driving in a major snowstorm. Luckily, I had lots of freeze-resistant wiper fluid handy and was able to clean the windshield. Without it I would have been driving blindly on unknown roads. It doesn't take long in those situations for visibility to drop to dangerous lows. It's advantageous to have the right fluid on hand.

If you find yourself in bad conditions without washer fluid, you can improvise by using a lump of clean snow to scrub the scum off your windshield. This will at least enable you to see while you drive to the local auto supply store or gas station to buy more. It's better to have too much wiper fluid on hand than not enough!

### Battery & Fluid

Most batteries today are "maintenance free," which means you can't check the fluid levels. But that doesn't mean that they're always in perfect condition. It pays to occasionally look at the battery posts for dampness or corrosion around the terminals . If you see this occur, either clean the battery if you're brave and want to take the time (see pages 259–261 for instructions) or have it inspected by a mechanic right away.

I also recommend having a mechanic perform a battery starting/charging system analysis once a year to detect possible breakdowns in the system that may prevent your engine from starting. Most mechanics will do that for you for a minimal fee when you have your oil changed.

## *Filters*

This may sound simple, but the truth is when filters are dirty they need to be changed. A clean filter for your vehicle is like breathing pure mountain air. It makes its systems work much more efficiently. Changing filters is a very inexpensive procedure and essential to your vehicle's health. Filter contamination and degradation is determined by a multitude of factors, such as driving habits, driving environment, smog, parking conditions, and the type of gas being used. How frequently to change the filters differs among climates and automobiles. However, there are some standard rules.

### Oil Filters

We already discussed that you should change your oil filter every time you change your oil.

The K & N air filter on my T-bird. On the right, I'm removing the filter by carefully twisting it.

### Air Filters

Air filters are the large, round boxes that sit on top of carburetors in older vehicles. And in fuel-injected engines, air cleaners are covered by round or rectangular plastic covers and can be found in different places in the engine compartment. Air filters need to

Another type of air filter under its plastic cover.

be changed when they become clogged, which on average, is about once a year unless you live in an area with a lot of airborne contaminants, smog, and congestion. In these cases they will have to be changed more frequently. You can check your air filter by unscrewing the wing nut on the lid or the fasteners on the plastic cover of the air cleaner, removing the air filter and holding it up to the light. If light shines through the filter, it's in good shape. If not, while keeping the filter face up, try hitting it gently against the ground a few times. If light still does not shine through, it's definitely time to replace the filter. You can purchase the right filter for your ride at an auto parts store or your dealership.

### Fuel and Crankcase Filters

It's more difficult to check fuel and crankcase filters. I suggest having them checked by a mechanic during bi-annual tune-ups. Typically you should change your fuel filter every thirty thousand miles, but this can vary depending on the quality of gas you use.

### Belts and Hoses

When doing periodic checks within your engine compartment and underneath your vehicle, look to make sure there aren't any leaks, and also do a visual inspection of the belts. Are the belts worn, ripped, or cracked anywhere? If so, they will need to be replaced. During tune-ups a mechanic will look for wear and breakdown of the rubber belts, while checking for radiator and washer fluid leaks. Timing belts need to be replaced at intervals ranging from 30,000 to 100,000 miles, depending on the model of vehicle you drive. Not all cars have timing belts, and V-configuration and horizontally opposed engines have multiple timing belts.

## Ignition System

Some ignition components, like spark plugs, will deteriorate with regular wear. This varies widely by vehicle make and model, and you will have to either rely on your manufacturer's guidelines for replacement intervals or ask your mechanic. It's a good idea to have a technician check your ignition system during tune-ups. Most repair shops, and these days even local oil change centers, have ignition analysis equipment that will quickly verify that everything is in tip-top shape. This is the more complicated part of engine mechanics.

Many car models make it difficult for even the educated owner to do ignition system maintenance. I have a friend who owned a pony car that had to have its engine block pulled just to access the spark plugs. In addition to the fact that the plugs are often located in hard-to-reach places, positioning them correctly is also tough and requires precision. You need a special wrench and a set of gapping tools to remove the old ones, check them, and replace them. The spark plugs can easily break if you don't grab them correctly, possibly leaving you with half a spark plug stuck in your engine and a nasty repair bill. Spark plugs need to be replaced methodically and one at a time, while the engine is off and completely cool. No dirt or debris should touch the spark plugs or wires. So really, for this one, you're off the hook! It's just better to use a mechanic.

I'll give you a quick overview of spark plugs so you'll have a better understanding of their placement and function. In an inline four-cylinder engine, the spark plugs sit in a row along one side of the engine. In a V6, V8, or V12 the spark plugs are located on both sides of the engine. There are an equal number of spark plugs and cylinders. At the head of the spark plug is a small piece of metal folded over an electrode that connects through a wire to your distributor, and from there connects to the top of your distributor cap. Here, the wires flow to the coil, then to your car's battery. Electricity flows through this system to the spark plug, which creates a spark at its head when the piston is fully compressed and gasoline vapor is sitting in the cylinder at its head. *BOOM!* The gas vapor ignites, explodes, and pushes the cylinder all the way down. That's the beautiful sound of power, baby, and it's where the basic mechanical energy of your engine comes from—millions and millions of little explosions, each set off by a spark from your spark plugs.

When the spark plugs get older, they get residue in them, making the sparks less reliable. Your engine will start to run rougher, and maybe even begin to stall. If you notice this happening, it's a good idea to have a mechanic check your spark plugs, as they may need to be replaced. Other than that, the ignition system is complicated, and I don't really recommend you check it yourself. While it's important to have an understanding of the system, unless you have the proper tools and experience, I suggest leaving this work to the pros.

A closer look at a modern fuel injection engine.

## *Fuel System*

Besides the fuel filter, the fuel injection system and the intake valves also need regular maintenance. You should have them cleaned every fifteen thousand miles under normal driving conditions and more frequently if you're demanding a lot of your vehicle. If you race, do a lot of stop-and-go driving, or drive in extreme heat, you'll want to check the entire fuel system more often.

## *Tires*

There's an entire chapter on tire maintenance later in this book. But I'll make an important point here that I cannot stress enough. Be sure to check your tire pressure regularly. Grab your gauge from your glove box and check the pressure at least once a week. It should take less than two minutes and will save you money, help the environment, and could even save your life. Trust me, it is so important to do this!

### *Brakes*

If you neglect your brakes they will ultimately fail, and you definitely don't want that happening while you're driving. Although brake pads cost a few hundred dollars to replace, it's essential to keep them in top condition. Maintaining brakes properly will not only help keep you safe on the road, it could also save you money in the long run by eliminating unecessary repairs. If the pads wear too low, damage can be caused to other, more expensive brake parts, such as rotors and calipers. You should have your brake system inspected every twelve thousand miles for wear under normal driving conditions and more often if you race, spend a lot of time in traffic, or drive frequently on hilly terrain. Coincidentally, the Ford dealership in L.A. is actually changing my brake pads and rotors as I write this, and they are estimating it'll cost about three hundred dollars for the job.

Brakes come in two types. The more common are disc brakes, and some older vehicles still have drum brakes. Disc brakes usually have a wear indicator embedded into them. When the brake pads wear down to the point that driving is unsafe, you will hear a nasty high-pitched squeal indicating you've waited too long to get the pads replaced. If you hear that noise, you should see a service center and get them replaced immediately. But I hope you don't wait that long! While brake pads are fairly inexpensive, the rest of the components in the system are costly.

Drum brakes don't have wear indicators. When the pads have

I had just removed this rear end from a Bel Air during *Overhaulin'*.

Helping to deconstruct a '63 Falcon

worn you will hear a horrible grinding noise when you apply the breaks. By then, it may be too late to replace only the brake shoe. Chances are other damage has been done, and you may need to replace all the brake components. Ouch.

You will find other maintenance recommendations in your owner's manual. Refer often to your maintenance log to ensure you're keeping your ride in optimum shape. A little maintenance along the way will prevent monster repair bills later. Maintenance alone will not guarantee that nothing ever goes wrong with your car, but it is your best hope of prolonging your vehicle's life and keeping yourself and others safe on the road.

**Why do American-made cars use the metric system for measuring engine size instead of the standard system that was used in the past?**

Since many imported cars are sold in the American marketplace, and many American cars are sold overseas, American auto manufacturers began using the metric system to measure engine volume, giving the figures in liters, rather than cubic inches. This way, when American, European, and Asian car buyers were comparing engine displacement across several vehicle models they were comparing them on a standard system.

**What do the acronyms SS, GT, and R/T represent?**

Super Sport, Grand Tourismo, and Road & Track.

**Why is it so important to keep mufflers and exhaust systems in good shape?**

You want to keep them in good condition because of the danger of carbon-monoxide poisoning. Annually there are fourteen thousand single-car accidents involving fatalities for which there is no explanation. Many of these deaths are believed to have been caused by carbon monoxide poisoning. It's important to have your vehicle's exhaust system inspected twice a year during tune-ups. If you have a damaged muffler or tailpipe, it could be emitting toxic fumes. If you suspect this is the case, it's a good idea to drive as soon as possible to a service center to have your exhaust system checked. Signs that you may be experiencing carbon monoxide poisoning while driving are shortness of breath and a headache.

**I typically leave my house on business trips for months at a time. Do you have any tips for the proper way to store my car?**

There is definitely a way to properly store your vehicle in order to keep it in the best possible condition. First, make sure both the fuel tank and oil reservoir are filled. You actually want to top off all fluids. The lack of open space in the tank and reservoirs helps prevent corrosion or rust particles from forming that can cause damage to your engine. Also, disconnect the battery so that it doesn't drain while you're away. When covering your ride if it's left outdoors, make sure the cover is clean on the inside, or small dust pieces could become like a cyclone underneath the cover and cause serious damage to your paint job. Finally, store your vehicle on a flat surface to both prevent liquids from being at an angle and possibly draining out, and to keep the weight evenly distributed on the four tires.

# FLUID FUNCTIONS

**F**or a lot of you, the only fluid you might think about putting in your car is gasoline. And while gas certainly is important, there are a plethora of other fluids that make the engine, all the systems, and many of the features in your vehicle function properly. Basically, with the exception of the tires, which separate the turning wheels from the road, fluids insulate every other moving part in the engine. If you've ever walked through an auto supply store, you know that the sheer number of automotive fluid products and brands available is pretty impressive! Here's a list of the most common ones that are needed to operate your ride:

1. gasoline
2. motor oil
3. radiator fluid/antifreeze
4. windshield wiper fluid
5. transmission fluid

Some of the information in this chapter was covered in the previous chapter. However, I felt it was so important that I should include it here as well in case you're skipping around!

6. brake fluid

7. power steering fluid

8. battery fluid

Each of these fluids has its own reservoir within the engine compartment (except the fuel), and almost all come in several different varieties and viscosities. The many vehicles on the road have separate needs. It's important to familiarize yourself with your manufacturer's recommendations for what fluids are best for your particular make and model in order to ensure you're maximizing your car's performance and life.

Let's take a brief look at each of these fluids, their function, and where each reservoir is located.

### Gasoline

It used to be that the only thing that was universally true about gasoline was that all cars needed it. With today's alternative fuel technologies even that's no longer true. As mentioned earlier, some vehicles operate on electricity, others on alternate fuels. We are also exploring the possibility of hydrogen. Still, more than 99 percent of the vehicles on the road have gasoline engines and need regular fuel fill-ups to run.

Now, how to put fuel in a car may seem like a "no-brainer" to most of us. However, I have been approached by women who asked me what type of gas to use and how to put it in their vehicles. For some women, the men have always handled the trips to the gas station. So I'm going to summarize the basics and offer a few tips for finding the best fuel for your ride. On most cars the gas cap is located near the back of the vehicle, on one side or the other. In some older cars and trucks, the gas cap is located beneath a flip-down license plate on the rear bumper. Some gas caps also require key access. The key is often the same as the ignition key. If you have a keyed gas cap on a ride you're driving for the first time, make sure you have a key that unlocks it. Most gas cap doors are activated by an interior release, and some don't require a key or release button.

*Always* stop the engine before filling the gas tank. In some states this is required by law. It is dangerous to add fuel while the engine is running because a spark from your engine could ignite the gas vapor from an open fuel tank. While you're at the pump, it's also important to extinguish all smoking materials for the same reason. It's also a bad idea to talk on cell phones while at the pump because they can ignite gas fumes as well.

All service stations now sell two primary types of gasoline—diesel and unleaded. Even though some older vehicles will run on leaded gasoline, it is no longer sold commercially, and performance of those cars will not be hindered by burning unleaded fuel. *Never* put diesel fuel in a non diesel engine or vice versa. The diesel pumps at service stations are usually clearly marked and generally have a different-colored nozzle than unleaded fuels.

At most stations, you will have three choices of unleaded fuel. Each will have a number designation. The lower the number, the lower the octane. High-octane, or "high-test," has a very high rating and is considered cleaner. However, not all cars require, or even benefit from, using higher-octane gas. Experts agree that only high-compression, turbocharged, or supercharged engines require high-octane. So if you're driving a stock 4-cylinder compact car, high-octane gas is really just a waste of money.

Some mechanics recommend that you run at least one tank of higher-octane fuel every three fill-ups. The higher detergent content will help clean any residue in your fuel system. I believe midgrade gas is sufficient for this. And while cars that demand premium fuel will run on lower-octane fuel in a pinch, it's a bad idea for long-term use.

Over time, many engines will develop knock. Knock, also known as detonation, sounds like a pinging or knocking noise as the engine runs. It's the result of abnormal combustion in your engine. Sometimes running a higher-octane grade of gas will stop it for a period of time, providing a great short term solution. However, prolonged knock will damage pistons and bearings. So if you hear these sounds, you should definitely have a mechanic take a look at your engine.

Knock-Knock. *Who's there?* A mechanic. *A mechanic who?* A mechanic who will fix that knocking sound if better fuel doesn't do the trick! (Sorry, couldn't resist that one.)

Some cars these days come with a flexfuel option. This means they can run on a fuel made of 85 percent ethanol, rather than gasoline. These fuels are becoming more commonly available and are made from corn rather than petroleum. Using such fuels reduces our dependence on imported oil. Almost all cars can use a fuel that has 15 percent percent ethanol content. But consult your owner's manual to be sure that your vehicle is capable of using fuels with a higher concentration of ethanol.

I know people who use filtered french fry oil in their diesel trucks instead of gas. One guy stops weekly at Carl's Jr., picks up their used fry oil, filters it, and adds it to his gas tank, combining it with a couple of gallons of diesel fuel to help it start better. He didn't modity his engine to do this, he gets several more miles to the gallon, and he saves a lot of money! Stacey David, the former *Trucks!* host, also demonstrated how to convert french fry oil to diesel fuel during one of his episodes. Pretty amazing stuff!

In case you missed this tip earlier, it bears repeating: If possible, try to avoid filling your vehicle when the station is receiving a delivery of fuel. The full-size tanker truck at the station with the hoses and lines pumping gas into an underground tank is a dead giveaway. All fuel tanks, even in delivery trucks, have some water content. Over time, the station's underground reservoirs will have built up water and sediment. When the gas and sediment have settled into the tank, the heavier water and impurities will sink to the lowest point, which means the fuel you're pumping into your car is much purer than what's on the bottom. While the station's tank is being filled, the water and gunk in the bottom mixes with the gasoline that's being pumped. If you fill your tank during this process, you will likely get small amounts of water and sediment mixed in with your gas. While this probably won't seriously damage your engine, it will mean that your fuel isn't "dry," or pure. This can be especially troublesome in the winter when low temperatures may cause the water to freeze. If the water freezes in a crucial area of a gas line, your vehicle may not start, because the ice will block the flow of fuel to the engine.

For this same reason, it's important to keep your tank at least half full during the winter months in cold climates. This limits the amount of condensation in your gas tank, which helps keep water out of your fuel and prevents any freezing.

If you do have water in your fuel tank, there are several gas treatments (such as STP, Heet, and Iso-Heet) available that can help purge it from the gas tank and engine before it causes trouble. Check your owner's manual to see if the manufacturer recommends one in particular. In general, it's a good idea to add a bottle of gas treatment to a full fuel tank once a month. It will help your engine run smoother, dryer and longer.

## *Motor Oil*

There are almost as many different choices of motor oil as there are flavors of soda pop. Oil is mostly sold in quart bottles in automotive supply stores, service stations, and large "'big box" stores. Mechanics' opinions vary widely as to the best oil brand out there. I suggest asking a mechanic you trust or going with a familiar brand.

The series of numbers and markings that designate what type of oil is in the bottle are regulated by the American Petroleum Institute (API). The API assigns letter ratings to motor oil. The category ratings correspond to industry standards for various qualities like viscosity, thermal protection, and the ability to prevent large deposits and sludge. Currently the highest API rating is SL. An SL on your bottle indicates that the API has judged that maker's product to be of the highest possible quality that meets the best performance standards.

There are multi-viscosity oils and straight weight oils. Viscosity refers to the weight or consistency of the oil. Multi-viscosity oils use additives and polymers to change the natural consistency of the oil as its heated. This prevents the viscosity from breaking down. Consider what happens when you heat a slab of butter, another type of oil. Chilled butter is obviously a solid. As it warms it becomes softer and begins to lose its viscosity. At room temperature, it's stirrable. As it gets warmer, it begins to liquefy. When very hot, it's runny. Motor oil reacts to heat the same way. Straight-weight oils thin as they heat, like butter. Multi-viscosity oils don't thin as much in the heat and are, generally, better for your engine.

A multi-viscosity oil will have a designation on it that consists of two numbers with a *W* in between them—such as 10W-40 or 10W-50. That *W* used to stand for *winter* back when not all oils were rated for seasonal wear. Winter oils, or multi-viscosity oils, were developed to withstand vast temperature ranges. These multi-viscosity oils are almost exclusively used today rather than straight-weight, or monograde oils. The only drawback to this is that some of the additives used to improve viscosity at high temperatures can also leave sticky deposits. Manufacturers have tried to eliminate the stickiness by adding detergents to oil. Most modern oils also include rust inhibitors and antioxidants. Some precise performance engines will still require straight-weight oil, but unless you drive a Formula-1 racecar, your vehicle probably requires a multi-viscosity oil. Failure to use one will void your warranty, and that is definitely something you want to avoid. One thing is certain; keeping the proper type and amount of oil in your vehicle and changing it every three months or three thousand miles will dramatically increase the life of your ride. It's an inexpensive process that could nearly double the life of your engine.

The numbers on a bottle of oil refer to the viscosity or thickness of the oil. The higher the number, the thicker the oil. The numbers themselves are supposed to correspond to a set of real, measurable qualities in the oil, one of which is the viscosity index. In multi-viscosity oils, the left number refers to behavior of the particular oil in the cold, while the right number refers to its behavior in hot temperatures (above 100°C). For example, 5W-30 oil would flow well when cold like 5-weight oil, but protect at high temperatures like 30-weight oil.

However, it gets a little confusing, because these numbers aren't necessarily standard. Oils vary widely by brand. The 5W-30 oil from one company might equal 10W-40 oil from another company in viscosity. This happens despite API regulation, because there are differences in other properties of the oil, for example the flash point, or temperature at which the oil ignites. Again, your owner's manual will tell you the kind of oil that is best for your vehicle, and I suggest choosing a reputable brand. As your car ages and the gas mileage hits the high digits, many experts recommend changing to a thicker oil. When you reach the hundred thousand mile mark, you definitely want to change the weight of your oil. Over time, gaps between parts in the engine become larger, preventing oil from reaching all critical parts. There are specialty products for high mileage vehicles at the auto parts store, and you might consider giving them a try.

*Never* mix different brands or weights. If you want to switch weight or brands, wait until an oil change, and remember to replace the filter as well.

### Synthetic Oils

Newer technology has brought us synthetic oils. Synthetic oils are generally better than multi-viscosity and straight-weight oils, but they are also more expensive. They can offer stronger high-temperature resistance and better low-temperature flow, and they claim to leave nearly no deposits. They won't break down as quickly and will allow you to travel many more miles between oil changes. Synthetics do cost a little more, but their prices are coming down, and there are also blends that combine synthetics with traditional mineral oils. Because synthetic oils flow and penetrate better than regular oils, a change to synthetic oil will sometimes reveal leaks you didn't know existed. Do not mix synthetic oils with regular oil unless it comes that way in the bottle.

## *Radiator Fluid/Coolant (AKA Anti-freeze)*

The radiator is located behind the grill at the front of the vehicle. The fill cap is located on the top of the radiator. The radiator and cap are extremely hot when the car has been running. The steam that pours out when removing the cap could severely burn your skin. Except in an emergency, *never* open the radiator until the engine has cooled. If you must, use adequate protection to keep your eyes, face and hands from getting burned, and stand back as far as you can when removing the cap and adding fluid.

Shortly after our crew "stole" an Oldsmobile 4-4-2 during an *Overhaulin'* episode, the car overheated on the Los Angeles 405 Interstate on the way back to the garage. We had no choice but to stop and buy a few bottles of water to use in this emergency. However, we had to make sure that the water we were adding to the radiator was room temperature, because pouring cold water into a vehicle's hot radiator can actually shock it and crack it, leading to very expensive repairs. (It's important to be sure that your car and your coolant are at roughly the same temperature when you combine them.) As soon as we got the 4-4-2 to the shop, we immediately replaced the water with the proper coolant mixture.

While the radiator will work with regular water in a pinch, it's not recommended. Use a coolant that is rated for your type of vehicle and your driving conditions. Some coolants have greater anti-freeze properties than others. If you live in an area where temperatures routinely drop below freezing, you should use a higher anti-freeze solution.

Checking your coolant levels is fairly easy. On the bottom of the fill cap there may be a dipstick with a fill-level indicator, or there may be a transparent plastic reservoir with a marking on it for the recommended maximum and minimum fluid fill levels. If you have a dipstick, unscrew the cap and check the level. If you have a translucent reservoir, eyeball the fluid level. If it's low, top it off. Be sure to replace the cap after checking or filling the fluid. Failure to do so will cause the radiator to steam and will rapidly deplete the amount of coolant in the tank, which is terrible for your engine.

An important tip about coolants: They have glycol content that gives them a sweet taste that pets may find appealing. Even a small amount of coolant can be fatal to an animal. Though some manufacturers have so-called "low-tox" coolant mixes, that simply means that it takes a larger amount to injure or kill the pet. Please don't take any chances! Clean any messes left on the street or driveway immediately.

The bright green color of coolant might also be appealing to children. While children are not as likely as pets to enjoy the taste, even one experimental sip is a bad idea. It's best to be certain to clean up all coolant spills right away and keep bottles tightly capped and far away from pets and children. As with other chemicals in your home, introducing a "Mister Yuk" label (the guy with a nasty-looking face that indicates it's not a tasty substance) or similar warning label system onto the bottle is a great idea. And if you have a coolant leak, get it fixed as soon as possible. That little puddle of coolant you leave behind may be a poisonous trap for some unsuspecting innocent.

## Windshield Wiper Fluid

Most cars have a button somewhere on the wiper control gadget that, when pushed, will spray wiper fluid onto the windshield to facilitate cleaning. I assume you're familiar with this! While regular water will work in the system, it's not as effective as a solvent with the proper cleaning agents. Certain driving conditions will cover your windshield with gunk that requires a washer fluid with tough cleaning agents to get rid of it so you can see well and drive safely.

After it snows, melt-off from the snow and ice mixes with dirt, oil, and other road debris to cause a sticky, slimy mess that could quickly limit your visibility. In certain conditions, you could find your visibility cut to almost nothing. All washer fluids contain cleaning agents that help dissolve this kind of residue. And fluids that are designed to sustain the winter months have anti-freeze properties, which remain in liquid form during freezing weather.

You will also need washer fluid in areas that have a lot of bugs, especially during certain times of the year. If you've ever driven in the south during bug season, you know what I mean. After just a few miles of driving, particularly in the evening, there will be a mess of smeared bugs covering the entire windshield. Water alone won't remove that mess. It takes washer fluid with strong cleaning agents. My dad was always a stickler about making sure our cars were free of bugs on both the windshield and paint job. He explained to us that the sun will bake the bug splatter into a vehicle's paint and could potentially ruin it.

You'll also need more washer fluid if you live on rough country roads or in the desert where there is a lot of sand or dirt, or in major cities where pollution creates a film that covers the windshield.

It's quick and easy to fill your windshield fluid reservoir—and what's more, it's really inexpensive. So you have no excuse! Solvent is usually sold in gallon jugs and costs less than two dollars. I recommend carrying some in your car when you're driving, especially in conditions where you'll be using the fluid more liberally.

The location of the reservoir can vary by vehicle, but it's going to be under the hood, and it's usually closer to the driver's side of the vehicle in a translucent plastic tank. It probably even has a little symbol with wipers and fluid on it indicating what it is.

When filling the reservoir you want to make sure to leave enough room for the cap to screw or snap back in place. It's ok to mix different brands of windshield wiper solvent. Just make sure that the kind you get is best suited for your driving conditions.

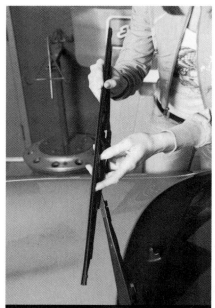

Wiper blades are easy to change yourself.

Windshield wiper blades should also be replaced periodically, especially if you live in a rainy climate where you use them more frequently. Failure to change them will not only affect the job they do in clearing the windshield so you have proper visibility, but the exposed metal blades could scratch your windshield, potentially leading to very costly repairs. Wiper blades can be purchased at auto supply stores, gas stations, and big box discount stores and generally cost less than $15. I change them myself very easily and it takes just a couple of minutes. If you don't want to change them yourself, ask an attendant at a full-service gas station.

Here's a quick tip to help lengthen the life of your windshield wiper blades: If you rub high grit sand paper along the edge of the worn blades, it will expose the softer material underneath and make the wipers work more effectively.

## Transmission Fluid

Most modern cars have "maintenance free" transmissions, which basically means that you can't check your own transmission fluid because there's no reservoir under the hood. Your owner's manual will tell you whether or not you have a transmission fluid reservoir. If yours does, you should plan on checking the fluid levels at least once every thousand miles for the first five thousand miles you drive your vehicle. If levels seem to be holding, you can plan on checking your transmission fluid every time you change your oil.

If fluid levels are dropping, there may be a leak, and you should have your transmission checked by a mechanic to prevent costly transmission trouble later. Before adding fluid, make sure you purchase the appropriate kind for your vehicle. Different transmissions require different fluids. Automatic transmissions use automatic transmission fluid. Manual transmissions use a variety of fluids, such as regular motor oil, heavyweight hypoid gear oil, or automatic transmission fluid. Some vehicles recommend specific brands. Your owner's manual will tell you what fluid is best for your transmission.

## Brake Fluid

The brake fluid in your brake system allows pressure to be evenly distributed from the master cylinder through the brake lines to your brakes when you press the pedal. The right fluid levels are essential for proper brake function and safety.

The brake fluid reservoir is located under the hood. Your owner's manual will indicate the exact location and tell you the recommended fluid for your vehicle. I suggest that you ask a mechanic to check the brake fluid level during every oil change and right away if your brakes are squeaking or feel unresponsive. Squeaky brakes could be a sign of low fluid or worn brake pads. It's important to find the problem right away so it doesn't become a more costly issue later.

## *Power Steering Fluid*

The hydraulic fluid in your power steering system is what makes it easy to steer your car. The reservoir is located under the hood and usually has a symbol of a steering wheel on it. Without power steering fluid, the wheel would be very stiff and difficult to turn. Most modern cars come with the power steering function. Over time, the seals and o-rings of the power steering system can break down, leaving tiny pieces of rubber in the system. This causes the pump to work harder and eventually fail, which is extremely expensive to repair.

Checking power steering fluid levels takes more than a quick look because the fluid is contained within the complex system. It's a job I recommend leaving to a mechanic. There are some signs, however, that will warn you that fluid levels are low. Levels might be low or there may be a leak if the power steering becomes unusually loose, if you notice a whining or groaning noise when turning the wheel, or if you find a leak beneath the car. Although it's possible to add fluid for a temporary fix, chances are it will deplete quickly as a result of a bigger problem. It's possible you need an o-ring replacement to repair a leak, which is much cheaper than a failed power steering pump. Leave it to the pros to figure out.

I learned about the loss of power steering fluid when I borrowed a friend's car during a summer in Florida. He told me he had an issue with his power steering system, and he was right. I had to stop at different gas stations every half an hour and talk with service technicians who helped me add transmission fluid to the reservoir as a temporary solution, because I could hardly steer without it. When a mechanic finally had time to inspect the system, he found that all it needed was a new o-ring. Fixing that early would have saved a lot of time, money, and hassle.

## Battery Water

Most modern batteries do not require fluid checks. Familiarize yourself with the battery in your vehicle and find out if it needs to be checked regularly for fluid levels. If you see frequent or excessive corrosion around your battery terminals, it needs to be checked for leaks, whether the battery is sealed or refillable.

## Other Fluids

There are other fluids, such as differential fluid and HVAC fluid, which help make your vehicle run properly as well. I recommend spending some time familiarizing yourself with where all these fluids are and what systems they control and facilitate. It's always beneficial to recognize signs of trouble, resolve the issues right away, and prevent hefty repair bills later. Most quick-lube places will check all of your major fluids at each oil change. Ask them to do this for you. Seasonal fluid checks are also a good idea.

Your car will enjoy better health and longer life if you properly maintain all of its fluid levels!

# TIRES: WHERE THE RUBBER
# HITS THE ROAD

**W**hat's the big deal about tires, you ask? Why devote an entire chapter to them? Well, the answer is that tires are one of the most important components on a vehicle, and yet statistics show they are also the part of the car or truck that drivers neglect the most. Numerous studies, including one commissioned by AAA in the United States and another by the Canadian government, prove this.

Tires, with their small mass of rubber and air, are the only part of your ride that touches the road. Tires are a large factor in determining that every stop, start, turn, swerve, and any other action the car tackles is done safely. National Highway Traffic Safety Administration (NHTSA) statistics indicate that more than a third of the vehicles on U.S. roads have at least one improperly inflated or dangerously worn tire. Can you believe that? Not only does this endanger the driver, passengers, and all others on the road, but under-inflated tires also wear out much more quickly and cause the vehicle to guzzle gas, which costs you money!

In 2003, more than twenty-three thousand auto accidents were caused by vehicles with poor tire conditions, and every year five hundred people in the United

With Chip Foose, Al Valor, and one of Chip's beautiful wheel designs.

States are killed in incidents resulting from improperly maintained tires. AAA alone receives more than three million calls a year from motorists stranded with tire problems, and many other roadside assistance companies issue similar reports. The amazing thing to consider is that these eye-opening statistics could be greatly altered if we all practiced some fast, easy, and inexpensive tire maintenance.

In the following sections I'll walk you through the process of checking your tires both visually and with a pressure gauge and explain how you can read and understand their numbers and tread. If all of you will begin conducting these simple tire checks, we will be doing our part in keeping the roads safer, preserving our vehicles and the environment, and saving ourselves money.

The safety factor alone is quite an incentive in caring for tires. But the benefits certainly don't stop there! In fact, proper tire care has many big advantages. Keeping your tires in good condition will improve your vehicle's handling and could boost its gas mileage by as much as 25 percent. Considering today's hefty and rising gas prices, this will save you a bundle on fuel. Driving with properly inflated rubber is proven to actually double the lifespan of a set of tires for the average driver. Consumers have a wide variety of tire choices today. Some tires can get as much as 80,000 miles but only with regular, proper maintenance.

A standard set of tires for a small passenger vehicle costs around five hundred dollars, and that price rises significantly for high-performance or low-profile tires, and obviously when equipping an SUV, truck, or luxury vehicle. Keeping the tires properly inflated while owning a standard car can easily save you more than three thousand dollars between extended tire life and improved gas mileage (the average driver will save two weeks worth of gas annually), and it's more than twice that amount for an SUV.

Proper tire maintenance will also aid the environment by reducing greenhouse gas emissions and cutting down on the number of prematurly worn out tires each year.

With all of that in mind, let's look at these unsung champions of the road!

## Getting Acquainted

Did you know that, if you get down on your hands and knees, it's likely that more of your body's surface area is in contact with the ground than your tires have rubber touching the road? Now think about your ride speeding down the highway at seventy miles an hour on that little bit of tread!

Did you know that 95 percent of the weight of your car is carried only by the air in your tires?

Did you know that many filling station tire gauges are inaccurate?

Did you know that a tire has its biography written on it, and it can be easily deciphered?

The first and most important thing to understand about your tires is whether or not they are properly inflated. Since standard tire pressure for passenger vehicles can vary from twenty pounds per square inch of air pressure (or PSI) to sixty PSI, guessing won't

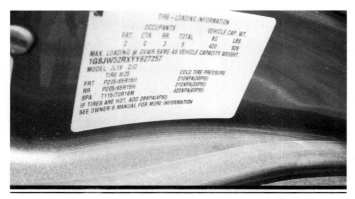

A sticker like this shows the ideal tire pressure for each tire on your vehicle.

don't do the job. But the good news is that in at least two different places on your vehicle, the manufacturer has listed the recommended tire pressure for your ride. Common places to check include the owner's manual, the B pillar (the area between the driver's and rear passenger door), the back of the visors, inside the glove box, and inside the trunk. The PSI listed on the side of the tire normally indicates the *maximum* weight the tire can withstand, or maximum PSI, so you don't want to follow that number when adding air for daily driving.

To check your tire pressure, you'll need a tire pressure gauge, and I recommend purchasing your own rather than using the one at a station or borrowing one. You can't really trust the gauges at filling stations because they're used so frequently and tampered with. Also, they get rolled over by everything from kids' bicycles to eighteen-wheelers, and you can't be certain how conscientious the station's owners are about getting the equipment calibrated. So it's better to buy your own, pick one that you can read easily, and keep it in your glove box. They're inexpensive, and you can find them at auto parts stores and most general stores.

There are many types of tire gauges. Some are digital, some have dials, and some look kind of like a pen and have a little stick that pops out to indicate the correct pressure. The gauge you choose is a matter of personal taste. Lately I've been using the stem gauge with the stick that pops out.

You want a gauge that reads to at least 60 PSI—not that you want your car's tires to be filled to that pressure, but because you will most likely need one in that range to check your spare. The average inflation pressure of the compact spare in most passenger cars is 60 PSI.

Now that you have your gauge, it's time to check the tire pressure in all *five* of your tires. (Don't forget that spare!) Be sure to check prior to driving, when the tires are at the same temperature as the ambient air. The air in your tires heats up as you drive, so measuring pressure after the car has been moving will give a false and (excuse the pun) inflated reading.

Have you ever noticed how NASCAR drivers' tires look slightly deflated when they're sitting on the grid at the start before the race? This is because the mechanics are overcompensating for the fact that the tires will quickly inflate at high temperatures during the race. As soon as the rubber hits the road at high speeds, the tires begin to expand. If the drivers started the race with tires set at the standard air pressure for daily driving, the tires could explode.

It's important to check your tire pressure at least once a month (I actually recommend weekly), whenever there's been a drastic change in temperature (because tire pressure is affected by changes in the ambient air), and before leaving for a long road trip.

All tires will naturally have a little air leakage over time. But in addition to this, there could be a steady leak of air caused by a tiny hole in the tire, a leak in the valve stem, a bent wheel that's allowing air to escape, a puncture wound, or a nail in the tire. You'll want to detect the cause of the leak and address it right away. Replacing tires is expensive.

Keeping the proper tire pressure is so important that the federal government is getting involved. Congress passed a law in 2000 that mandates tire pressure monitoring systems in all new vehicles. NHTSA promulgated a regulation in 2004 to phase in this requirement. Beginning with the 2008 model year, all new vehicles are required to have tire pressure monitoring systems. However, even if your car is equipped with a tire pressure monitor, it's still important to check tire pressure every month with a tire gauge. The system will only warn you when tire pressure drops 25 percent, which is a substantial loss of pressure and could lead to tire damage if driven on for long periods of time.

It's a good idea to check tire pressure again every time temperature or driving conditions change. The very best time to do this is in the morning, before getting in your car and driving. It takes me less than two minutes. Come on, you can give your car a couple of minutes every few days!

Now, eyeballing tires to guess their pressure doesn't work. Nor does the time-honored tradition of kicking them. A tire can be thirty percent under-inflated before it starts to look low, and it can be over-inflated to the bursting point yet look perfectly fine to the eye. Radials like the ones on my T-Bird, for instance, sometimes look low on air or flat when they are really at the correct PSI.

Many people have stopped to tell me I have a flat when all four tires are at the perfect pressure. A good tire gauge is the only way to ensure an accurate reading.

Many of you probably already have the tire pressure checking process down. Congratulations, you can skip right past the following section. For those of you who *haven't* yet done it, your hands may get a little dirty, but I find it sexy to get dirty while tackling auto maintenance. Just be prepared to wash your hands afterward. Or even better, use the hand sanitizer and a paper towel from your emergency kit when you're finished.

I also demonstrated this two-minute tire pressure check on the *Tyra Banks Show.* The young woman who attempted the check after me thought it was a breeze. I think you will too.

1. Grab your gauge.

2. Open your owner's manual or the driver's side door (and look at the B-pillar) to get the recommended PSI for your ride

3. Locate the valve stem on the first wheel you plan to check, and remove the cap.

4. Place the gauge firmly on the stem so that it's flush and press down hard enough so that there's no sound of air leaking from the connection. (You'll hear it hiss if you don't have the gauge lined up properly. The hiss means your tires are losing pressure).

5. After you get a good connection, read your gauge and compare it with the recommended PSI number. (If using a stem gauge, be sure to reset it after checking each tire.)

6. Either release air by pressing the gauge lightly on the valve stem until air hisses out of the tires or add air using a compressor or bicycle pump in order to get the reading closer to

the recommended pressure. If you don't have a mini air compressor or a bike pump at home, you can find air at most local service or gas stations. Driving for a short distance won't alter the air pressure very much.

7.  Check the pressure again. Repeat this process until the air pressure is correct.

8.  When you have the correct pressure in one tire, replace the valve stem cap, and move on to the next one.

9.  When all four tires are the correct pressure, congratulate yourself.

There are a number of possible options to install on your vehicle if you want to monitor tire pressure. The lowest priced aftermarket option is a set of replacement valve caps with built-in pressure indicators. The caps display yellow tops when the tires are starting to slip out of the ideal PSI zone, and red tops when the tires are significantly under-inflated. Other systems monitor tire pressure constantly on a small screen that attaches to the dashboard.

The next part of the tire check is a visual inspection of all your tires. Did you know all that writing on the sidewall of a tire tells the story of its life?

## The Writing on the Wall

This section gets a little technical, and the information may not be critical for everyone to understand. But here's how to decipher the language on the wall of your tire.

When you look at the tire, it will generally have the manufacturer's name on the sidewall, along with a group of letters and numbers.

You'll notice a *P* or *LT*, which stands for either passenger car or light truck. (FYI, your spare tire will probably have a *T* on it, which stands for temporary spare). You'll also notice some numbers. The first three-digit number is the tire cross-section width, measured in millimeters. The next number, generally two digits, is the aspect ratio. That is the height of the sidewall. A lower number indicates a wide tread area relative to the sidewall, while a higher number means you have a taller, thinner tire.

An *R* indicates that your tire is a radial. These days, radial tires are pretty much standard equipment on all passenger vehicles. If it's a radial, you may also see a *B* or a *D*, or in rare occasions, an *E*. *B* stands for belted, *D* for diagonal bias, and *E* for elliptic. I told you this was technical, but some of us dig this stuff.

Another two-digit number gives the measurement of the wheel's diameter in inches—generally this measurement runs between 12 and 18 inches for passenger vehicles. However, rappers seem to like 20 or 22 inches. If they don't like them, they sure sing about them a lot!

There is yet another two-digit number following the size information, which is a load-versus-pressure rating. There's an industry-standard chart that measures how much load each type of tire can bear. This chart ranges from 65, which stands for 639 pounds, to 150, which stands for 7385 pounds.

Usually, the maximum pressure and weight load indicated by the chart are broken out and written on the tire next to the rim. It's important to note that the tire pressure indicated on the side of the tire is often the maximum the car can withstand at that load rating, or it will give you a range. Again, you don't actually want to inflate the tire to that maximum number. The same holds true for the load indicated. Just because your tire reading indicates it can carry 1,600 pounds, it's not necessary to test that assertion.

The letter that follows that two-digit rating is the speed rating.

An *S*, which is typical for most passenger vehicles, means that the tire is rated safely for speeds up to 112 mph. The ratings go from *A* to *Z*, with *Z* being the best. *Z* tires are safe for speeds above 149 miles an hour. I smile every time I see a *Z*-rated tire on a car I'm about to test-drive. Growing up in a racing family, I got very familiar with the *Z* rating.

You'll find maximum pressure (in PSI and kilopascals), and maximum load (in kilograms and pounds) written around the tire rim.

You'll also see numerical or letter grades for the tire's relative tread life, traction, and temperature variables. Of course, this information can vary due to the make and model of tire, but it's fairly standard over most passenger tires. There's something called the Uniform Tire Quality Grading system, or UTQG, that sets national standards. All tire makes and models are compared to that standard, and the results are there on the tire for you to read.

The first number is the tread wear ratio. The baseline for an acceptable tire, according to the UTQG, is 100. A car rated 200 for tread wear will last twice as long as that minimum rating, and so on.

Traction is rated by the UTQG on a scale from *A* to *C* with *AA* being the best. Traction is the ability of your car's tires to grip the road. Thankfully, my tires have *AA* traction, which makes me feel safe when maneuvering on the fast freeways and windy L.A. roads. That is when I'm not going two miles an hour in bumper to bumper daily traffic. Sometimes in L.A. the freeways are jammed even on Saturday afternoons. I constantly have to remind myself that the many amazing things that drew me to L.A. drew all of the others, too.

The ability of a tire to sustain high temperatures is also rated using a scale from *A* to *C*. Again, *A* is the best rating. It you live in the South, make sure your tires are rated *A* for temperature. In Florida, our family's tires were always rated *A*.

Most tires these days are rated "All-season," indicating that they are designed to be left on the car year-round and can withstand most climates. There are also some specialty tires on the market that are tailored for driving in extreme climates and terrains. "Winter" tires are one type available for those who drive in heavy snow and ice and on unplowed roads. Growing up in Northern Minnesota with snowstorms and a dad who ice raced, I'm definitely familiar with these. "All-terrain" tires are designed for people who do a lot of off-roading. For most of you, however, "All-season" tires will be sufficient.

The letters DOT should appear on your tire sidewall somewhere with numbers following them. DOT indicates that the Department of Transportation has certified the tire model. The first numbers represent the week of the year it was made, and the last two represent the year. For example, if the tire reads "DOT 4003," this means that the tire was manufactured in week 40 of the year 2003.

### Tread Talk

Now that you're fast asleep. . . . just kidding. Now that you know how to decipher the sidewall of the tire, it's time to inspect the tread to be sure the tires meet safety standards.

With every mile you drive, you're actually writing a story on your tires. The way that tires wear can tell you a great deal about your vehicle's condition, your driving habits, and your attention to keeping your rubber properly maintained. It's a good idea to periodically inspect the tires for any issues or changes, especially after putting your tires through any trauma. For example, if you scraped a curb, drove over an obstacle, went through a construction zone where you might have picked up a nail, abruptly stopped to avoid an animal in the road, etc., you may have in some way injured your tires. It's a good idea to get down by your tires and inspect each one right away. Look for any rips, gashes, asymmetrical bumps, or swelling. If you notice any of these issues, bring the car to a service center or tire shop for repair right away, rather than waiting for the problem to get worse. Ignoring a small issue could mean the tire becomes unsalvagable, a rim could be bent, or you could find yourself in a roadside emergency.

While inspecting your tire, also rub your hand along its surface. It should feel smooth. If you detect a rough texture, this most likely indicates that your car is out of alignment and your tires are wearing unevenly. It's a good idea to visit a shop to have the alignment corrected.

Don't freak out if you do find a problem area. If the sidewall is in good shape, some small punctures on the tread area (less than one-fourth inch in diameter) can be patched, saving you money and extending the life of your tire.

In addition to keeping proper pressure and checking tires for any issues, it's also important to monitor your tires' tread depth and wear. In order for your tires to grip the road properly, they should have at least one-sixteenth of an inch of tread. A quick and easy tip for checking this is to place a penny with a Lincoln head between the tread, with the top of Lincoln's head facing down into the tread. If you see all of Lincoln's head, your tire's tread is dangerously thin. If you want an exact tread reading, there are also tire tread gauges. But I prefer the penny trick because it's easy and free.

I recommend testing each tire in three places; in the middle and along each edge. If the tread is one-sixteenth of an inch or deeper in all three places, the tread on your tire is deep enough. If the tread is shallower than that, it's time to get new ones because they don't have enough grip to keep you safely on the road.

Get down on your knees and examine the tread wear on each tire. A healthy tire wears evenly, with the tread in the middle *slightly* thicker than the tread at the edges of the tire. If the tire has excessive wear on the outside edges of the tread, it means you've been driving with your wheels under-inflated. If the tire has excessive wear in the middle of the tread, it means you've been driving with your wheels over-inflated. Monitoring your tire pressure and keeping it at the correct PSI will avoid these problems! After you've detected the issue, go ahead and add or remove air to bring the PSI to the proper number.

All passenger and light truck tires have tread wear indicators, which are solid bands that appear in the tire tread when you've worn your tread below that one-sixteenth inch limit. If you've been inspecting your tires, you'll catch the problem before the tread-wear indicators show. And that's important, because driving on tires that have the indicator bands showing could lead to substantially reduced traction and therefore dangerous driving.

If a tire is worn more on one side than another, it is misaligned, and the wheel is probably set a bit off, or with excessive "camber," as we say in the industry. If this is the case, the wheels and tires probably need to be realigned. If you notice that there is excessive wear in any one spot, your tires need to be rebalanced.

If you have bald spots appearing in a regular scalloped pattern in your tire's tread, the tires are out of balance *and* misaligned.

At any signs of irregular tire wear, I'd have the vehicle and tires

An under-inflated tire. (The tread on the outer edges is more worn.)

An over-inflated tire. (The tread on the center of the tire is more worn.)

inspected at a service station or tire center. Most garages are equipped to handle tire repairs, but for tire replacement and vehicle alignments, I suggest going to a tire specialist.

In addition to regularly checking your pressure, tread and doing visual inspections to ensure that your tires are in the best possible condition and safe for driving, you should also have your tires rotated every 5,000 to 7,000 miles. When servicing your vehicle, ask the mechanic to rotate your tires. If you bring your car in for oil changes every 3,000 miles (rather than tackling the job yourself), you can also ask to have the tires rotated during every other visit. The vehicle's already on the lift, so it's the perfect time to take care of it. It's a quick, easy process, so the mechanic will probably be willing to do it for a minimal fee. If you visit the center where you purchased your tires, they will likely rotate them free of charge. Check before you purchase them to make sure that tire rotation is included in the agreement.

If you are a total stud and are rotating the tires yourself, be aware that there is a difference in the way you rotate radials versus bias-plys. Radials are rotated from front right to rear right and front left to rear left. Also, be sure that your rear wheels and tires aren't bigger than the front. On many muscle cars and high-end sportscars, the rear tires are slightly bigger or wider. In this case, obviously, rotating is not a possibility. Check your owner's manual for the proper rotation pattern for your vehicle.

Also, when purchasing tires, you should never mix bias-plys and radials. If you are in a dire situation and there is no other option, put the radials on the rear wheels. However, never put a radial and bias on the same axle.

When tire shopping, I recommend both looking for good deals on name brand, quality tires and purchasing those that come with a warranty and free rotation. There is also the option to add road hazard insurance to your tires, which is designed to protect you from any unforeseen, abnormal road conditions that could destroy your tire.

In chapter 21 I'll walk you through a tire change, a task I'm confident you all can easily conquer yourselves!

Treating your rubber right takes very little time and will keep you and your ride safe, preserve the life of the tires, aid the environment and save you money. Nothing like a win, win, win, win. Wooo hoooo!

A tire with dangerously thin tread.

## *Beyond the Standard Radial Tire*

Most of the new vehicles coming off the auto manufacturer's assembly lines come with radial tires, and low profile or sport packages are offered for an additional upgrade fee. These sportier and fancier tires appeal to consumers who are looking for better handling at higher speeds, enhanced performance, and more flash. The tires have a lower profile, meaning you see more wheel than tire, and the tires are wider. They are becoming increasingly popular today. According to industry experts, high performance tires are the single biggest trend in tire sales. Manufactures have recently quoted up to 20 percent growth margins in the sales of these tires.

Before upgrading to a bigger wheel and a lower profile tire, you should know that they can cost two to three times what standard radials cost. And you can't get these tires without also purchasing appropriate wheels, which cost even more. And finally, be aware that the life expectancy of these tires is often significantly less.

Also, with bigger wheels and lower profile tires, the vehicle's ride height is lower, which does make for a different driving experience. Though the special wheels and tires look cool, give the car a sporty right height, and handle unbelievably at high speeds, the trade-off is that you will spend more money often feel every nook and cranny in the road.

### Run-Flats

Many tires on luxury and high-end sports cars come with the run-flat system. Run-flats have self-supporting tires and special rims. They have reinforcement built within the tire that ensures that, in the event of tire pressure loss or a flat, driving is possible for short distances at low speeds, allowing you time to get to a garage for repair. However, I have heard that if low profile tires get a flat, continuing to drive can cause the wheel to "eat" the tire, which would mean repair is unlikely, and the tire will probably have to be replaced.

I highly recommend doing your research thoroughly and considering what you're buying carefully before making a purchase that could cost you a big initial investment and more money down the road.

Is the "flash" worth the cash? That's up to you. For me, it is!

My T-Bird rolls on twenty-inch Foose Speedster wheels that are wrapped in high performance radials. It rides low to the ground and looks incredibly cool. I get maximum handling and perform-ance from the tires, and I love them!

I was feeling a little "tired" during an *Overhaulin'* build, so I took a break outside Foose design.

# MAINTAINING THAT "SHOW CAR" APPEAL

**W**hen it comes to people, it's what's on the *inside* that counts. With cars, the inside is definitely important too. Most of us like an impressive, power-packed engine compartment. And it's hard to beat that new car smell and feel. Sliding your booty behind the wheel of a vehicle that just came off the lot, new or used, is so much more satisfying than driving a grungy ride filled with food containers, note-books, and gym clothes.

However, with cars, looks are equally important. There's no denying that the vehicle's contours and lines accentuated by a stellar detailing job gleaming in the light had some affect on your purchase decision. Inside *and* out, your vehicle made a big initial impression on you. Well, there's no reason why your ride can't remain in the pristine condition of its early days. A little time and love will go a long way in protecting your car and keeping it looking and feeling like brand new.

Here are ten tips that will help you keep your ride in tip-top shape.

**1. Detail your car within the first weeks of purchase and at least once**

**annually thereafter (I prefer every six months).** I can't stress this enough. Detailing isn't only for aesthetics. It also helps protect your paint job, wheels, and interior. Find a good detailer who offers reasonable prices (solid detailing jobs typically run between $100-$200; yes, it's a hefty sum, but you're only doing it once or twice a year!), and take your car in for an interior and exterior cleaning and detailing within the first few weeks. The dealer or owner may not have done the same comprehensive job a professional will do. A dealer might be satisfied with cosmetic appeal, while a detailer will do a thorough job inside and out.

Make sure the detailing includes an exterior wax, which protects your car from road grime, bugs, corrosion, and other pollutants that damage the paint finish over time. Cloth interiors should be treated with a stain protection coating. Leather and vinyl need to be treated to prevent fading and cracking caused by sun and heat. And wheels should be treated for protection and shine.

Because you're forking over a fair amount of cash for a detail job, you have the right to be particular. Don't be afraid to ask a lot of questions about what's included in the job, and always look the car over well to be sure you're completely satisfied before driving away.

Let me add that although it's definitely a good idea to detail your ride once or twice a year, if you live in an area where there are heavy road pollutants or you drive where there is a lot of dirt or sand, you may want to do it more frequently. Because of L.A. sand and smog, my T-Bird gets treated to a detail job at least every four months.

If you aren't cool with spending the money to have your

ride detailed, go ahead and attempt it yourself. But be sure to get quality, name brand waxes and cleaners and micro-fiber or chamois rags designed for detailing that aren't going to scratch your paint job.

2. **Treat Your Ride to a Hand Wash Once a Month.** If you feel like giving your car a good old-fashioned cleaning in the driveway, go for it. (Women, you may even have fun cranking some tunes and incorporating a few Jessica Simpson or Paris Hilton moves!) Just be sure to use the proper cleaning products and non-abrasive rags and towels.

   People often ask me if it will hurt a paint job to use dish soap or other household cleaning products on their cars. I say, why take chances? Use the cleaners that are formulated for cleaning autos. There are a plethora of products available that are inexpensive and easy to find. If you have custom graphics or decals, be sure to check with the manufacturer or painter to ensure that you know how to properly treat the surface.

   If you don't choose to wash your car at home, there are soft touch, or "brushless," car washes where the work is done mostly by hand, using non-abrasive equipment and towels. Automatic commercial washes that use beaters and brushes are too tough on your paint job. If you can't find an automatic car wash that is brushless, I suggest finding a hand washing venue that comes recommended, and make sure they are being gentle with your ride.

   My family owned a car wash and detailing center in Florida many years ago, and from working there I learned firsthand how essential it is to hand wash vehicles regularly inside and out in order to keep them both beautiful and well protected. If you can afford to wash your car more frequently than once a month, even better. I wash the T-Bird every two weeks.

In case the "brushless" hand washes don't remove hidden grime found beneath bumpers, inside wheel wells or stuck to your paint surface, here are a couple of home remedies. When removing tar or pine sap, apply a small amount of cooking oil with a cotton towel, or a soft clean shop rag, or leave a dab of petroleum jelly on the area for a few hours. Then wipe it gently away. To remove tree sap, gently rub on a small dose of mineral spirits before washing. For removing bird droppings, my mom especially likes the trick Kevin Tetz, the host of *Trucks,* taught during a recent episode. He suggests using a homemade mixture of 1 tablespoon baking soda and 1 quart warm water. Stir until the baking soda dissolves, then dampen a microfiber cloth with the mixture and gently blot it on the spot until it loosens enough to come up. Be careful to blot and not rub here, because there could be rocks or seeds in the dropping and you don't want to scratch your car's finish by rub-

Polishing my wheels with my favorite 3M tire and wheel cleaner.

bing them in. After you've loosened the dropping rinse it off using a microfiber cloth with just warm water. All of these tricks have worked for me. There are also special cleaning products available specifically for treating these issues, but I find it more fun to be resourceful and thrifty.

By the way, it's a fallacy that rain water cleans cars. Rain contains pollutants and contaminants from the environment that will make your vehicle even dirtier. Also, snow-melt chemicals found on busy roads will eat at your paint job and cause rust to form. I actually suggest washing your ride after a rain.

3. **Take care of scratches and dings ASAP.** Minor scratches and dings can often be buffed out by a good detailer. If you attempt to do the work yourself, be sure to use the proper buffing cream, equipment, and non-abrasive cloths.

You can also ask your dealer if they have a paint repair kit. But be sure to follow the directions carefully. They also sell touch-up paint pens for cars at auto parts stores. The pens aren't going to match your vehicle's paint color exactly, but they will do the trick. Chip Foose taught me that for a quick cosmetic fix you can cover a tiny paint scratch or ding with the appropriate colored Sharpie marker. When I first got my T-Bird, I was preparing for a photo shoot with *Celebrity Car* magazine. The night before the shoot, a white truck backed into my car's hood, taking a gouge from the paint. I freaked out and called Foose. He told me to use a black Sharpie to color over the metal and white paint until I could have the ding properly repaired. The T-Bird was perfectly presentable for the shoot!

Leaving scratches and dings for long periods of time not only looks bad, but can lead to rust and corrosion which will eat at your paint job and lead to more costly repairs later on. If you have major paint and body damage, please don't delay in having it repaired. The paint-free metal will rust when exposed to water, and rust is your car's enemy!

4. **Maintain a proper following distance on the road.** I know this is tough to swallow for you speedsters out there, but keeping the recommended six car lengths between you and other drivers is more than just a safe driving tip. Not only could you plow into the driver ahead of you in the event of a sudden stop, but flying road debris could pose a serious hazard to your vehicle. If you're following too closely behind other drivers, any airborne debris could strike your vehicle and damage your windshield or paint job. It's a good idea to give the vehicles ahead of you a wide berth, especially when following utility hauling trucks, dump trucks, and open container vehicles. If they're driving too slowly, I maneuver around them as quickly as possible, obeying the speed limit. Even the covers on these vehicles (which are required in most states) won't prevent tiny rocks or other debris from flying through the air. At seventy miles an hour, little pebbles have the impact of a .22 caliber bullet! You don't want to find *that* one out the hard way.

5. **Choose parking spots wisely.** If at all possible, avoid the spaces designated for "compact cars" in parking garages and lots, even if you drive a compact car. Those spots are extremely narrow and might lead to door dings by drivers who try to squeeze in too closely. My cars have suffered a few accidents over the years because of this, so I learned the hard way. Also, if you park close to a post or wall, make sure you have enough room to get in and out safely, and be careful when opening doors. All those paint and tire marks on posts and walls weren't put there intentionally.

   Try to park your vehicle far away from other cars, even if it means a slightly longer walk. Have you ever noticed how a beautiful sportscar will be parked far away from all the other vehicles in a lot? Chances are you'll never find a Bentley or Aston Martin jammed between two other cars in a parking structure. Your ride deserves the same respect. Also, never park beside a vehicle that's dinged or beaten up. If you have a choice, park next to the car that's newer and nicer, and hopefully the driver will respect your ride as much as his or her own.

When parallel parking, try to leave at least a foot between your vehicle and the ones parked in front and in back of you. Drivers will try to squeeze in too tightly and could rub your bumpers, damaging your paint job. Also avoid getting too close to sidewalks and curbs, as you could scrape your wheels and gouge your tires, which are both costly to repair.

As a reminder, when more people are in a car the added weight lowers the vehicle. So make sure passengers are cautious when opening their doors to avoid dragging them on the sidewalk and scraping the paint job.

If you can, park in the shade. But try to avoid fruit-bearing trees or those with falling leaves and branches. Also avoid parking under telephone wires, as perched birds might decide to leave you a messy little surprise.

6. **While loading and unloading things into your vehicle, do not rest items on top of your car.** When getting into your vehicle, place suitcases, groceries, tools, cell phones, baby seats, and other items on the sidewalk, rather than setting them on the surface of your ride. Not only will they scrape your paint, but you might forget about them and drive away, causing the items to break, be destroyed, or hit another vehicle. I've heard countless stories about this, and here's one of

my own. Just last week, I was about to drive somewhere with a friend, and he put his hat, car keys, and ipod on top of my car, thinking they would be there for just a few seconds. Well, I think putting stuff on top of a car causes amnesia, because two seconds later he forgot about it, and we drove off. People in other cars tried to alert us. He even got out to make sure the tires were ok and the taillights were working. Nothing was wrong, so we didn't understand what they were saying. A half an hour later, looking for his ipod and hat, he remembered that he left that stuff on the roof! Suddenly the people who were screaming at us made sense. But it was too late. His stuff had flown off and gotten crushed by oncoming traffic, and he eventually had to tow his car to the dealership to get a new key made. I also busted his chops because he could have damaged my paint job. Have I made my point? Please, don't put stuff on top of your car.

7. **Take care of windshield pits and cracks immediately.** A tiny crack in your windshield can spread quickly, which is not only dangerous but a violation of the law. Many insurance companies will waive your deductible if you use a repair service to take care of the chip before it becomes a major issue. If you notice a crack, take your car to a windshield specialist right away.

8. **Treat all interior surfaces once a year and vacuum often.** If you aren't having your car professionally detailed regularly, make sure to treat the cloth, vinyl, and leather surfaces yourself. Also vacuum your vehicle's interior often to protect carpets from unnecessary wear caused by sand and dirt, and take care of any spills as soon as they occur.

9. **Don't use your car's interior as a trash receptacle.** I know with busy lives and hectic schedules it can be difficult to maintain a tidy interior. It's easy to get complacent through the daily grind and allow things to pile up and become cluttered. But you should really try to keep the inside of your ride clean, because not only is your car a reflection of you, but sharp objects or items getting lodged behind seats could damage your interior. Besides, your car deserves to look good! Just make it a habit to take any junk out of your ride every time you get out. If you let it stay there once, you'll do it again, and before you know it you are driving around in an expensive, moving garbage can.

10. **Clean the engine at least once every six months.** For all you extreme car junkies who want to do all of the maintenance yourself, here's how you keep your engine as pretty as the rest of your ride. Choose a degreaser and engine cleaner that you feel comfortable with and be sure to follow the manufacturer's instructions before applying them. A clean engine not only looks terrific, but makes finding small leaks easier, runs cooler, and extends the life of your car.

    You can also cover your carburetor, if you have one, and the spark plugs, and have your engine steam cleaned or pressure washed.

Pressure washing an *Overhaulin'* ride.

# WARRANTIES AND REPLACEMENT PARTS

*U*h-oh, there's a funny smell coming from your vehicle. Or you notice a strange noise while driving. Or there's an oil spot on the driveway where you parked last night. Or your car won't start. . . . At some point during your relationship with your ride, no matter how much you love it, the road is bound to get bumpy. But this is unconditional love, remember? Part of your relationship with your car or truck means caring for it during those inevitable times of trouble.

Here are some tips that will help get you through tough times:

1. **Be familiar with your car's warranty.** As I mentioned earlier in the book, warranties are great because they limit your own personal cash loss on auto repairs and help bring you peace of mind. You should be familiar with what your warranty covers, how long it's in effect and what the restrictions are on utilizing it. If your car encounters a problem that is covered under warranty, you should definitely take advantage of that and visit your dealership service center for the repairs. There are many advantages to using your dealer for

233

repair work. If you have the work done elsewhere and it's done incorrectly, your warranty could be voided. Your dealer will also have the most current information about your vehicle from the manufacturer regarding any recalls, which could be taken care of at the time of repair. The dealer's knowledge of your vehicle's onboard computer diagnostics can also save time. The onboard computer will quickly inform the mechanic of the source of the problem. In most cases, the warranty will also cover the labor fees associated with the repairs if you make them at your car dealer service center. All warranties are different, but good ones cover most repairs, outside of tires, for several years or somewhere between 50,000 and 100,000 miles. Be aware that some manufacturers offer extended warranties, which can really be a money-saver as your car gets older. Also, when tricking your ride, be careful that you do something that will void your warranty.

2. **Watch for recall notices.** Even if your warranty has expired, if your vehicle's repairs are associated with a recall notice, those costs will be covered by your dealer. Your auto manufacturer will send you a notice informing you of any recalls for your car or truck. So, if you move, be sure to give your dealer your current address. If you want to check to see what recall notices are out there for your ride, there are a number of Web sites that keep full listings of auto recalls. One of them is the National Highway Transportation Safety Administration at http://www-odi.nhtsa.dot.gov/cars/problems/recalls/recallsearch.cfm. That's a long web address to type in, so you probably want to bookmark it!

3. **What to do after your warranty expires:** If you're happy with your dealership service center, it's probably easiest to con-

tinue using them for service and repairs even after the warranty's expiration. My T-Bird's warranty expired, but I continue to use the Ford dealership for all service and repair needs. If you would rather look elsewhere for a mechanic, I recommend doing some research and asking friends, family, and coworkers for the name of a service center or mechanic they trust.

4. **Always get a second opinion before major repairs.** For big repairs, I highly suggest getting at least two different estimates. This will ensure you aren't being ripped off by inflated prices. My friend recently visited a mechanic and got a quote for replacing her starter. She had done some research and thought his price seemed high, so she got two other estimates. Her instinct was right, and the starter was replaced for much lower than the initial quote. You also want to be sure that what a mechanic is claiming needs to be repaired or replaced actually does. If in doubt, go back to your dealer.

5. **Don't ignore problems; they will only get worse.** This is so important. Putting off necessary auto repairs could lead to catastrophically expensive repairs down the road. Please don't ignore those smells, noises, and warning lights! They indicate trouble that needs to be addressed. The other day my car was idling erratically and seemed ready to stall. About a minute into this, the little wrench symbol lit up on my dashboard indicating engine trouble. I pulled over and popped the hood to check on the problem. Sure enough, I noticed that the o-ring had come loose and the air filter had disconnected from the intake pipe. I was able to grab the K&N air filter and connect it back to the pipe, problem solved! If I hadn't been able to take care of the problem

myself, I would have taken the T-Bird to my mechanics at the Ford dealership at my earliest opportunity. Problems need to be addressed immediately.

*Note:* If you see steam coming off your hood on a cold, rainy day, that is completely normal. It isn't smoke, and it probably doesn't mean you're leaking oil or experiencing an engine fire. Heat from the engine may cause the cold rainwater hitting your hood to vaporize and cause steam to be emitted through the hood. You'll especially notice this while idling. If the steam seems to be excessive, or if you notice it when the weather is dry, check to make sure your oil cap is tight. If the billowing steam continues, have your car checked. Also, sometimes when adding oil, some may spill or overflow on the engine block. This could cause a little fire.

It would be nice if our cars lived forever without any engine failure or trouble. But in my experience, with vehicles both old and new, trouble is inevitable. I hope the above information will help make the journey a little easier.

## Consider Used Parts

Rebuilt parts are the generic medications of automotive repair. They can save you hundreds of dollars on costly repairs to components like your alternator or radiator. The Internet is a great tool for locating manufacturers of rebuilt parts. These parts can also be found in junk yards and through local mechanics. Ask your mechanic if rebuilt parts are an option, but make sure that using them won't void your warranty.

- REBUILT: Parts that have been completely disassembled, cleaned, and adjusted (usually by hand) to perform like new.

Any worn pieces (like bearings and brushes, in the case of alternators) are replaced. You can order rebuilding kits for certain parts if you want to do that work yourself.

- RECYCLED: Parts that are collected from older vehicles by salvage yards or parts brokers. You can get amazing deals on them, and it's a great way to find parts for rare models. However, these recycled parts might appear to be in good shape, but because they are used, there is no guaranteeing how well they will function. Be sure to check the return policy and any warranty before purchasing them.

- REMANUFACTURED: Remanufactured parts are essentially the same as rebuilt parts, but they have been rebuilt in a large-scale facility and often repackaged like new parts. For

With my good friend Camee Edelbrock. She's holding an intake manifold, and I'm holding a carburetor.

instance, parts that have been rebuilt on an assembly-line are usually termed factory rebuilt, or remanufactured.

- RECONDITIONED: Reconditioned parts are specialized parts rebuilt for older cars no longer in OEM production. If you buy that classic '65 Mustang, you'll soon become acquainted with reconditioned parts. Their quality often depends on the expertise of the builder. Proper reconditioning entails removing rust, repairing or replacing worn areas of the part, and innovative, customized repair work for pieces no longer made. If you own a classic, I highly recommend that you find a collector's club or online chat group for your specific type of vehicle. The fellow enthusiasts will help you locate good quality reconditioned parts. There are hundreds of these clubs on MySpace.

# FINDING A GOOD BODY SHOP

There are auto designers and manufacturers, and there are custom car fabricators like Chip Foose, Sam Foose, and George Barris, the ultimate artists in their field. Both create these aerodynamic sculptures we call automobiles.

The process of body work and painting is also an art form in that it takes time and care and precision to be done correctly in order to restore a vehicle to its original condition.

Ford built my car, Chip Foose tricked it out to fit my personality, and fortunately I found Lanzini Body Works to keep the body in shape.

When I look at my Foosed-out T-Bird gleaming in the sun, especially after a good detail job, I can't help but smile. I call her the "sexy shark" because she looks just like one with the shiny grill, sparkling chrome wheels by Chip Foose, and an elegant black shape. She's absolutely stunning. I'm sure you all feel this same kind of love toward your own rides. Now you just need to discover your own "Lanzini" for those unfortunate occasions when your baby gets injured. This chapter contains tips for finding your dream body and paint shop.

Cutting sheet metal on an *Overhaulin'* car.

Unless you are a paint and body expert, this is probably work you'll want to leave to the pros, because they have specialized equipment and years of experience.

Finding a shop that will do the solid body work you and your car deserve might take a little time, so I suggest researching in advance of an accident. Ask your dealer who they use, and ask friends, family, and coworkers for a shop they might recommend.

Another great way to meet paint and body specialists is by attending local car club shows or auto shows. Not only is it fun to walk around and check out the cool cars and trucks, but you will often be able to see the amazing work and designs of some of the premier craftsmen in your area. Even at the biggest shows that are crowded with nationally known names, the local pros will be represented. I try to attend as many of these as I can throughout the year. Not only does attending the car shows allow you to see different places and hang out with hundreds or thousands of amazing rides, but you meet wonderful people. Car people are some of the best!

As you cruise around a local show, keep an eye out for the people with local plates on their cars and local addresses on their signage, and ask them about body shops in the area. They are at the show to meet new people, show off their rides and get attention for their work. They are probably eager to talk about their cars and connections they have within the industry. If you get really lucky, they may even be body and paint specialists themselves.

Another idea for finding a reputable body shop is to visit a few local shops and ask the owner for recent references. If the shop is good, there should be plenty of satisfied customers willing to talk about the work done on their vehicles. There may also be vehicles in the shop lot that have been repaired, and you could check them out as well.

Yet another valuable tool for finding a reputable body and paint shop is the Internet. You can do a search for body and paint specialists, look at any photos they have showcasing their work, and then ask about them on chat boards or within online car clubs.

If you have the luxury of time, I recommend getting labor and parts quotes from at least three different shops. A bid that's exceptionally low may be a red flag. Typically, unless you have sterling references telling you the lowest bidder is the best one, I suggest going with the middle quote.

If you didn't take the time to research prior to an accident, in the time of crisis you'll have to find a repair shop pretty quickly. Your insurance company will provide you with a list of names. You should choose three companies from the list and take your vehicle to all three of them for estimates. Again, be aware of a bid that's especially low. The shop may be trying to cut corners on repairs. If in doubt, go with the middle one.

Body work is a complex process that requires experience, time, and care. Reputable shops will do thorough work. You want to bring your ride to a place that will replace body panels or, if the job only calls for repairs, never use body fillers. You want a shop that will take time to sand properly, mask well, and prime and paint in layers using factory-matching color. If you aren't diligent in your search, you could get burned by losing money and suffering disappointing work.

I really trust Lanzini Body Works in Huntington Beach,

Getting a '63 Falcon ready for paint.

California for my body work and paint jobs because each time I've brought my car in, whether for a small ding or after a major hit and run calling for a great deal of repair work, they return the T-Bird to me in perfect condition. But that recommendation won't do all of you guys out there much good unless you happen to live in the L.A. area. So you'll have to find your own local genius. What I really appreciate about using the same body shop over and over is that they're familiar with my car, they have the right paint in stock, and I have confidence that they would never do anything to my vehicle that they wouldn't do to their own.

Labor rates differ depending on where you live, the shop, and the level of experience of the workers. But good labor generally costs between $60–75 per hour. I'd question rates that are much higher than that.

Here's how to check the quality of body work in person, whether it's on a vehicle you're examining for purchase or one you've had repaired. Take a hard look at the following:

1. **Seams**—Make sure the seams between the various body panels and along the doors, trunk and hood line up straight and without large or uneven gaps. In vehicles with light-colored paint jobs, these seams between body panels are more obvious and detract from your ride's aesthetic. Not only will trunks and doors with unmatching seams look sloppy, but they may rattle or have difficulty closing.

2. **Interior**—I recommend seeing an interior specialist for re-upholstery or major work. In the event of an accident that

affects your interior, the body shop will more than likely collaborate with an interior specialist. You'll want to check the repaired areas, making sure the work is precise.

3. **Metal work**—Unless you are driving a rat rod (if you are, I'm jealous; those are some of the coolest cars on the planet), all welds should be smooth and sanded completely down, flush to the surface. You shouldn't be able to tell where the welds were. In addition, the metal should be machined into shape, not buried in Bondo or body filler.

4. **Finish**—You shouldn't be able to tell where the original finish ends and the repaired or restored finish starts—and this should be as true six months after you've had the work done as it is the day you drove it off the body shop lot. A finish can appear beautiful for a few weeks, and then months later look splotchy, faded or dull.

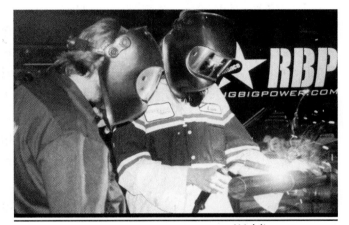

Welding at Magnaflow.

Don't wash your car for at least a week after having major body work done, and don't have it detailed for three to six months afterward. Ask the shop what they suggest.

Remember, your car is a reflection of you and part of your initial impression when meeting people. Don't you want it looking as nice as possible? I imagine you also want it to hold its value and be comfortable and safe to drive. It's important to seek out a shop that does solid work. You and your ride are worth it!

# HOW TO AVOID GETTING
# RIPPED OFF BY MECHANICS

*T*he most common question women ask me is how they can avoid getting ripped off when taking their car to a service or lube center. Though the tips on how to combat this problem apply to men as well, we women are the ones who need them the most. Because the automotive world is dominated by men, and most mechanics are men, I guess it's assumed we women know very little about caring for our cars and can therefore be taken advantage of at service centers. I recently saw a TV documentary that showed hidden camera footage taken from a day of work at a reputable lube center. The tapes showed that the service technicians weren't even changing the customers' oil! They were charging them but not doing the work.

Whether you're taking your vehicle in for a simple oil change, or your starter needs to be replaced, these tips will help you avoid being scammed.

1. If you want to have a little fun and **throw their chauvinism back at them,** I suggest making an appointment in a man's name. Although he won't be with you when you take your ride in, the service center will link him to the process, wonder when he might show up, and be less likely to rip you off.

2. **Do your research ahead of time.** If you think you need to replace your starter or get new brake pads, research the typical costs for those services. It's important to be informed so that you can speak knowledgably, using the automotive vernacular. There is a wealth of information online available to you at no cost. Take advantage of it.

3. **Dress respectably and walk in with confidence.** Body language in all facets of life says so much. Let the service technicians know you aren't intimidated and aren't going to be taken advantage of. Make eye contact, ask a lot of questions, and speak like the true auto enthusiast you are! Also, I don't suggest dressing provocatively. Although you may excite the men, they aren't going to respect you or take you seriously, and therefore they may be *more* likely to rip you off. Nothing is wrong with using a little charm and being attractive and fun. But turn on the charm while remaining a strong, respectable woman.

4. For major work like replacement of spark plugs, it's a good idea to **get a couple of estimates.** If you don't have time to visit different places, at least call two or three, including your dealership, tell them your make and model, and explain the problem. They should be able to give you a ballpark quote. In this case, I would go with the lowest quote or if the quotes are comparable, go to your dealership service center to have the work done.

5. **Ask for rates up front for both parts and labor, and compare them with the information you gathered.** I recommend always trying to negotiate rates down. Sometimes they will give you a deal on used parts or reduce the labor fees for you. Let the technician know you received other quotes, and after they give you their rate, tell them the other bids you received

were lower. If they balk and seem shocked, they are probably quoting you a fair price. There's nothing wrong with a little tough negotiating!

6. **Always ask the mechanic if rebuilt parts are available, and check to make sure that using them on your vehicle won't void your warranty.** If these parts are available and your warranty will remain intact, this is a great way to go. Rebuilt parts are cheaper and typically just as good.

7. If you go to the dealership where your vehicle is leased, be aware that they may try to rope you into excessive or premature repairs. They have an interest in doing all service and repair work possible on your vehicle, because if the dealer ends up owning your car or truck they want it in pristine condition to maximize its value for sale.

8. If a part on your vehicle is replaced, **ALWAYS ask for the old part back so you know they actually replaced it.** Also, inspect the new part on your car to make sure that it's actually new. If you have your oil changed, ask for the old filter back in a bag, and always check your oil afterward to make sure it has that new golden new oil sheen.

I'm so impressed with the growing number of female auto enthusiasts and the desire in the women I speak with to understand more about their cars and how they can take more of an active part in caring for them. I also think it's amazing when men aren't threatened by this, but rather embrace it and welcome us in the auto world. People always ask if I encounter chauvinism in the car industry. I'm proud to say that I have experienced none. However, I'm not proud of the scamming that goes on in service centers throughout the country. Let's all do our part to put an end to it! No more getting ripped off!

Removing the front clip of a '65 Mustang with my friend Jon Schultz.

# SPEED BUMPS AND PIT STOPS

Although many of you have AAA, OnStar, or other roadside emergency services, they may not always be able to get to you as quickly as you'd like, or you may not be able to call them if you're in areas without cell phone reception. Learning how to handle common roadside issues like flat tires, overheated radiators, and failed engines will bring you a certain peace of mind and could ultimately save your life. Besides, it's very gratifying to know how to tackle them!

Obviously, I can't predict or address every kind of emergency possible in the pages of this book. But I've been through enough of the common ones myself to be able to share with you what I've learned and offer tips on how to deal with some of them yourself.

## Flat Tire

Before finding yourself in a dire situation on some desert road with no AAA membership and a flat tire you don't know how to change, it's probably a good idea to practice changing a tire at least once at home. If you have a friend or relative who has done it before, invite them over to watch, laugh at you, and possibly offer helpful tips throughout the process. If your ride is brand new, it's also worth asking the dealer to show you how to change your tires with the onboard equipment as part of your orientation to the new car. Some dealerships even offer seminars that take you through the tire changing process for your specific make and model. Regardless of whether the dealer can help and how hardcore you want to be with this, you really should do a practice change soon after you buy your ride.

In the event of a flat, if it's late at night and you're a woman alone, trust your instincts and do what you feel is safe. You might feel more comfortable calling for help and waiting inside your vehicle with the doors locked. If you get a flat tire on a busy highway, especially at night, I definitely recommend calling for roadside assistance and waiting inside the vehicle. In this case it's a good idea to hang a white rag, towel, or piece of paper out of the driver's side window to alert the highway patrol that you need help.

If you decide to take care of the flat yourself, you have two options. You can use the Fix-A-Flat can in your trunk (more on this in the following section) or you can change the tire. I suggest keeping your cell phone near you while you're fixing or changing the flat because, in the unlikely case something more serious goes wrong, you'll want it handy to call for help.

Hopefully you've checked the pressure in your spare tire before this emergency so you know that it's in good condition. You should also have your emergency kit in the trunk full of the tools and items you need to change your tire. If you don't, you'll just have to make do with whatever's handy. Here are the simple tire-changing steps I believe you all can master. I demonstrated a tire change on the *Tyra Banks Show* in September 2006, and the young woman I instructed changed the tire perfectly on her first attempt:

1. **Drive your vehicle to the side of the road where the ground is level and you're away from oncoming traffic.** Driving too far on the flat could make the tire irreparable or bend the rim. However, the most important thing is your safety. Level ground will keep the car stable for conducting the tire change. If you get a flat on a hill and it isn't feasible to drive to the bottom, pull the car close to the curb, turn the wheels toward the curb, and then get out and block the downside wheels with wood blocks or metal chocks. You can also use books or any other creative resource to prevent the vehicle from rolling.

2. **Get your gear together.** Open your trunk and dig out your jack, the hollow pipe that fits over the jack handle for leverage (if you have one), a couple of rags or paper towels, your emergency reflectors and flares, your lug wrench, your wheel key (if you have one), a flashlight if it's dark, and metal wheel chocks or three pieces of wood. And don't forget the spare tire! Take the spare out of the trunk and roll it to the side of the vehicle near the flat tire.

3. **Put out flares.** In order to alert other drivers that you're in trouble, set out a lit flare and/or a reflective triangle from your emergency kit about ten car lengths behind your vehicle's rear bumper. (Ten car lengths is the average distance required for a driver to stop). Stagger the remaining flares and triangles along the road between that first flare and your car, but be extremely careful of oncoming traffic. Try to do this quickly. If you don't have flares and triangles, you can

raise the hood and tie a white rag or paper towel to your vehicle's antenna or hang a piece of paper out of the driver's side window.

4. **Put the vehicle in park with the emergency brake on.** With manual transmissions, make absolutely certain the E-brake is on.

5. **Secure the vehicle by chocking (blocking) the three good tires.** You never want to jack up a car without first chocking the tires, even if the vehicle is on level ground. Again, if you don't have the blocks or metal chocks, be creative.

6. **Remove the hubcap (if you have one).** Use a screwdriver or the flat end of your lug wrench to pry it off. You may have to work along the edge in a few different places. Set the hubcap to the side and use it to hold your lug nuts. It functions as a cup and will keep you organized. It really stinks to lose lugs!

7. **Loosen the lug nuts.** I assume you know what lugs are. They are the big nuts that hold the wheel in place. Now, it's much easier to loosen the lugs before jacking the vehicle because there is more traction with the wheel on the ground. You want to loosen them enough so that you can finish removing them by hand, but they should still be fastened firmly enough to keep the tire on the axle until you have the vehicle jacked up off the ground. I find that they are usually pretty hard to loosen. If so, step on the wrench handle to apply more force. It's best to work on the lug nuts in a cross-wise pattern. Loosen the top lug nut, then the opposite lug on the bottom of the wheel, then back to the lug nut next to the first lug nut, then the one opposite it, and so on. Loosening them in this pattern keeps the wheel straight and level.

8. **Position your jack properly.** You want to put your jack in

*exactly* the place recommended in your owner's manual. That place is usually marked by a notch or arrow on the car's frame. If you don't position it correctly for your vehicle, you could bend the frame while jacking, which is expensive to fix. Even worse, the vehicle could also come crashing down on you while you're working!

9. **Jack up the car.** Put the jack handle into the jack with its pipe extender, and raise the jack with smooth, even strokes of the handle.

10. **Make sure the car is stable.** Walk around the car and check to see that the other three wheels are chocked into place and completely stable. Then, standing back from your ride, give it a little jiggle to ensure that it is secure on the jack.

11. **Remove the lug nuts.** Finish removing the lugs by hand and set them together in the hubcap so you can easily find them again.

12. **Remove the flat tire.** The tire's going to be heavy and dirty, but I think getting a little dirty is healthy! Usually, the best way to remove the tire is to wiggle it gently and slowly until you are supporting the tire's weight, and it basically falls off. It's helpful to control the fall so the tire lands on its tread, but if you drop it don't worry. Roll the tire out of the way, in the direction of your trunk, where it will swap spots with the spare.

13. **Put on the spare tire.** Roll the spare over and lean it against your vehicle. Notice where the holes in the wheel are and match them with the screws. Lift the tire straight up and onto the screws. Wiggle the tire, as you push it firmly back until it fits against the axle and stabilizes.

14. **Replace the lug nuts.** Follow the same crosswise pattern you used when removing the lugs, tightening them now only *by*

*hand.* The wrench tightening will happen when the vehicle is back on the ground.

15. **Lower the jack.** Turn the jack handle counter-clockwise and slowly lower it until all four tires are resting solidly on the ground. Then pull the jack out from under your ride.

16. **Tighten the lug nuts.** Using the lug wrench and the spare pipe lever, tighten the lugs in the same cross-wise pattern until they are solid against the wheel. I also step on the wrench handle when tightening lugs to apply more force. You don't want to tighten them so hard that you strip or break the screws, but you also want to be sure the wheel is completely secure.

17. **Put the hubcap back.** Place the hubcap against the wheel and use your hand to push it firmly back in place. Don't use a hammer or tool for this, as you could easily dent the hubcap.

18. **Put your tire and jack back in the trunk where they belong.** Be careful when lifting the tire to use your legs, not your back. It will be heavy!

19. **Remove the chocks, put your tools away, hop in your car and drive carefully to the nearest service station or repair center.** Most modern cars have a small spare that will need to be replaced within fifty miles of your flat change. You shouldn't drive too fast (not over 50 mph) or too far (no more than 50 miles) on these tires. See your owner's manual for the recommended speed limit for your particular spare. It might also be listed on the side of the spare. Be sure to get the spare repaired or replaced and put back in the trunk.

20. **Congratulate yourself!**

It's a good idea to carry Fix-A-Flat in your emergency kit in case you find yourself in a sketchy location or it's late at night and you don't want to attempt the change. Fix-A-Flat will quickly seal the flat, inflate the tire, and allow you to safely proceed to a service station. But if you do use this product, be sure to inform the mechanic before he or she works on your tire, because the fumes from the substance are extremely flammable and will need to be ventilated. Fix-A-Flat is great for an emergency quick fix, but the downside is you won't be able to repair your tire at all. It will have to be replaced. Still, I recommend it in the event that it's not a good time or location to change your flat.

## My Car Won't Start

This one hopefully either means your vehicle is out of gas or your battery is dead, which are both relatively easy fixes. You should always be aware of how much gas is in your tank, and I recommend keeping it half full at all times. I used to be terrible about this in college but learned the hard way and now do my best to always keep the gas tank more than half full. If your car won't start, first check the fuel level.

If that isn't the issue, next check to see if the battery indicator light on your dashboard display is remaining on when you're attempting to start the car or truck. If so, the battery is probably out of juice. There is also an indicator eye on many batteries, which will turn black to let you know it's dead. In most cases, a dead battery will just need a quick jump (see pages 261–263). Now, if you haven't replaced the battery in a couple of years, you may be in need of a new one, which you can pick up at auto parts or big box stores, for anywhere from about $50 to $120, depending on the model of your size car or truck. Most batteries come with a warranty, and certain stores will offer a lower price for trading in the old battery, which is a great way to save you the hassle of disposing of the old one! Even if the indicator light isn't on, take a look at the battery. It's located either in the engine compartment or the trunk. Mine is in the trunk.

The battery in my T-Bird recently went completely dead. It wasn't jumpable. I looked up online what battery my car takes, went and purchased it for about $90, removed the old one, and installed the new one myself. If you realize that your battery is completely shot, I'm going to go over the steps for removing and replacing it. You will want to put on your leather gloves or the disposable gloves from your emergency kit before examining the battery because you might come in contact with battery acid, which can seriously burn your skin.

### Removing and Replacing a Battery

1. Most batteries have a clamp or holder that keeps it in place and prevents it from shaking. Loosen the nuts on that holder. If it has a cover, remove it.

2. Next, using a wrench, carefully loosen the positive (red) and negative (black) cables from the battery terminals. It doesn't make a difference which one you loosen first.

3. Then carefully remove the battery from the engine compartment. There is a special strap for removing batteries that can be purchased at auto parts stores. It's inexpensive and can be very helpful in doing this!

4. In the next section I'm going to tell you how to clean a battery. Before installing the new battery, you will want to clean the battery cables well. For this, use the baking soda and water mixture and a toothbrush or wire brush. If you don't

have baking soda and want to improvise, a trick I learned is to pour dark-colored soda pop on any corroded areas. The soda and battery acid cause a reaction that can dissolve that build-up.

5. Wait until the cables are dry and install the new battery, hooking up the positive (red) cable to the positive terminal and the negative (black) to the negative terminal.

6. If there is a holder or clamp on the new battery, screw that down. Replace the cover, if it has one.

7. This is very important! Be sure to conform with all environmental regulations when disposing of the old battery. Batteries contain lead that is toxic to the environment. I've taken mine to gas stations and they've kindly disposed of the battery for me. Auto parts stores will often do this as well. And when you purchase a new battery, the store will often take your old one.

If you replaced your own battery, you are truly a stud!

So, back to your vehicle that won't start. First, is it possible the battery could have frozen? Frozen batteries won't start, and it's a bad idea to try to jump them until they are thawed. In the case of a frozen battery, unfortunately you'll be out of luck if you're stranded on the side of the road. But if you're near a gas station or other warm place where you can carefully remove the battery from the vehicle and bring it inside to thaw, terrific. Let it thaw for about twenty minutes, and then put it back in the vehicle and attempt to start the engine.

If there isn't an indicator eye on the battery, or if the indicator reads that the battery has power, take a look at your battery cables where they connect to the posts. Are the connections loose?

Carefully tighten them, touching only one cable and post at a time. *Do not* touch both posts at the same time. You could get shocked. After tightening the cables, attempt to start the car.

If that didn't work, check to see if there is white corrosion on the ends of the cables. That could also be your problem. The corrosion is a result of acid build-up and needs to be cleaned so that the connection between battery and cables is solid. In an emergency situation away from home, corrosion can be temporarily removed using a screwdriver or other sharp tool by scraping it away. Wearing gloves when dealing with battery acid is a *must.*

To more thoroughly clean a corroded battery, you'll need to be stranded in your own driveway or near a house or business where it's possible to accomplish it. Cleaning batteries isn't difficult, but it's going to take a little time, because your battery should be completely dry before you start your engine after the white residue has been removed. To accomplish this you will need baking soda, water, petroleum jelly, an old toothbrush or wire brush, and your tool kit. Are you ready?

1. Mix a tablespoonful of baking soda with about a cup of water. Set that mixture aside.

2. Get a crescent wrench or a standard wrench of the appropriate size from your tool kit.

3. With your *gloves on,* unscrew the battery's case or hold-down clamp. DO NOT touch the positive post or cable yet. If you touch the positive cable or battery post while touching the negative cable or post, you could seriously injure yourself. Please be very careful!

4. Unscrew the negative (black) battery cable nut, and slowly

remove the cable from the battery. Once it's loose, set it down away from the battery.

5. Remove the positive (red) battery cable and set it down away from the battery.

6. Dip an old toothbrush into the water and baking soda mixture and carefully, holding the toothbrush only by its handle, use it to scrub the white corrosion off the negative battery post. Continue dipping the toothbrush in the water/baking soda mix as needed. It neutralizes the acid that caused the buildup. Scrub until the white stuff is completely removed.

7. Clean the negative cable end the same way, brushing and dipping until the white corrosion is gone. Set the cable aside to dry.

8. Clean the positive battery post and the positive battery cable.

9. Let everything dry *completely* (about 15 minutes).

10. Use a cloth to rub a small amount of petroleum jelly around the negative post. This prevents the metal from corroding again for a while. Then do the same around the positive post.

11. Reconnect the positive cable to the positive battery post and the negative cable to the negative battery post.

12. Reconnect the battery case or hold-down clamp.

13. Clean up your mess well, and remove your gloves, being careful not to touch any acid residue. Place the gloves, toothbrush and the container you used for your baking soda/water mixture carefully into a trash receptacle, preferably inside a plastic bag to keep any people or animals from accidentally touching the acid.

14. Now that your battery connections are solid and dry, attempt to start your vehicle again. If the battery has power, the engine should fire.

15. Congratulate yourself on being a mechanical little chemist!

If none of those attempts at starting your vehicle worked, it could mean that any number of things with your engine are wrong. Your battery might be completely dead and in need of replacement, you could have condensation in your fuel tank, your starter might be shot, etc. . . . Call an emergency roadside service company to help you, and see a mechanic at your first opportunity.

## How to Jump-Start a Car

Jump-starting a car is a quick, easy job that doesn't require gloves and leaves no messes. However, if it's done incorrectly, one or both batteries could explode, emitting battery acid, which is hazardous to you, your car and the neighborhood. It's important to be careful. I suggest taking a look at your owner's manual before providing or getting a jump. Certain vehicles should not be jump-started, and the manual will inform you if that's the case.

When looking for a vehicle to jump your ride, try to find one of comparable size and engine. A huge F350, for instance, could blow out the alternator and explode the battery of a 4-cylinder compact car. You also never want to jump a battery that has cracks in it or is leaking acid, as it could explode. If your battery is damaged, it's time to buy a new one.

Tyra Banks and I used two car batteries and jumper cables to demonstrate to her audience on the *Tyra Banks Show* how to properly jump a vehicle. It was a breeze and took only a couple of minutes. Here are the steps.

1. Grab your jumper cables or portable jumper. Make sure they're in good shape, with no exposed wiring or frayed insulation.
2. If the batteries of both vehicles are in the engine compartments, line the cars up engine to engine. If one battery is in the trunk (my T-Bird's is), while the other is in the engine

compartment, line the vehicles up engine to trunk. Just make sure the cars don't touch. If they touch, the electrical charge could short, preventing the jump.

3. Turn off anything that may be drawing juice from the dead engine—lights, radio, radar equipment, video games, DVD players, etc.

4. Make sure both engines are off, and put them in park (neutral with emergency brake on for manual transmissions).

5. Find the positive cables (the red ones), and make sure the cables are long enough to reach from one vehicle to the other. Clamp the positive cable to the positive terminal of the battery (marked with a plus (+) sign) in the vehicle that won't start. Clamp the other end of the positive cable to the positive battery post of the vehicle with the working battery.

6. Clamp the negative (black) cable to the negative battery post (marked with the (-) sign) on the working battery. Clamp the remaining end of the negative jumper cable to a piece of clean, unpainted, shiny metal (a nut would work great) somewhere on the engine of the car with the dead battery.

7. Wait for a couple minutes, and attempt to start your car. If the battery was in fact the problem, the engine should fire. If it does, give it a little gas and let it run in park for a few minutes. If it doesn't ignite, wait a few minutes and try again. If it still doesn't start, it probably means your battery is completely dead.

8. Unclamp the negative cable from the jumped car's engine, and remove the negative cable from the other vehicle's battery terminal.

9. Unclamp the positive cable from the good car's battery, and the positive cable from the jumped vehicle's battery.

Don't forget to thank the Good Samaritan who came to your rescue! They did their good deed for the day. Now it's your turn. And if you aren't sure why your battery died, I recommend taking your vehicle to a mechanic as soon as possible, even if you were able to start it. There may be an issue with your alternator. The alternator regenerates the excess electricity produced by your engine as you drive, feeding it back to the engine and keeping the battery charged. It may need to be repaired or replaced.

## Engine Overheated

If your engine overheats, you may be able to temporarily fix it and make your vehicle drivable. But after resolving the issue, I urge you to visit a service center. It will be much cheaper and easier to fix in the short term rather than waiting until a more serious engine issue happens down the road.

When you see the engine temperature gauge start rising on a hot day, immediately kill the air conditioning, open all of the windows, and turn on your heater at full blast. If the engine temperature decreases and returns to normal, your engine may have just been working too hard in the heat. The sudden rise in temperature could also have been due to a radiator leak, a closed thermostat, low oil or coolant levels, or a blown fan belt.

One very hot day I was on a road trip with a friend in the California desert hills, and his twenty-year-old car began lugging and overheating. We quickly rolled down the windows and cranked the heat, and we were able to give the engine a break and save it from failure. It was definitely uncomfortable for a few minutes. But we were happy to have avoided being stranded in that brutal heat in the middle of nowhere.

If the engine temperature doesn't drop when you kill the AC and crank the heat, or declines for a moment only to rise again rapidly, drive to the side of the road, turn off the vehicle, pop the hood, and let the engine cool. Be careful, because the engine is *hot*. You can tell if the engine is cool by holding your hand near the radiator. If you can feel heat coming from the system, it's still too hot to touch. *Do not* open the radiator cap until the vehicle is completely cool, or you could get terrible burns from the pressurized steam coming off the radiator. Once the engine has cooled, stand at arm's length from the radiator and slowly remove the cap. If there is no steam billowing from it, look and check the coolant level. If it's low and you have coolant in your car, go ahead and add it. If you don't have coolant, you can use lukewarm tap or bottled water. Cold water is detrimental to a hot engine and could cause serious damage. The sudden change in temperature can crack metal parts.

If the coolant level is normal, check the oil level. If it's low, and you have some oil on board, add it. If you don't have oil, do not attempt to restart the engine. Call for help because driving your engine when it's not properly lubricated will cause severe engine damage. In either case, have your vehicle inspected right away. Low oil levels could also mean a leak or crack in your oil pan.

Hopefully you are all now masters at handling common roadside emergencies.

# SOUPING UP AND TRICKING OUT

**Y**our ride is already a work of art, of course, but there's always room for more! There is a world of aftermarket tricks and add-ons that will make your vehicle tougher-sounding, more powerful, more comfy, more beautiful, slicker, safer, and more fun. Customizing cars and trucks makes them more of an extension of your personality. Car owners spend billions ($31 billion in 2005 alone) on aftermarket accessories. There is a multitude of options available, but I've come up with a list of several basic ideas for modifying your ride. All of these accessories are available through your dealer, your original equipment manufacturer (or OEM), online or in specialty stores.

The Specialty Equipment Manufacturers Association, or SEMA, holds many shows throughout the year. Their monster show happens annually in Las Vegas at the beginning of November. I attend the SEMA convention every year, and it always makes me red line. There are hundreds of thousands of fellow automotive enthusiasts who go, eager to check out the amazing, tricked-out rides and plethora of automotive parts and accessories available. SEMA's floors cover nearly *one mil-*

*lion* square feet. If you love your ride like I do, this is the show you should never miss. Hope to see you there!

Here are some ideas on how you can customize your ride and make it a SEMA-worthy show car:

### Dubs

"Dubs" refers to any wheels that are at least twenty inches in diameter. I'm rolling on Dubs with my Foosed-out T-Bird. There are wheels of all sizes and styles. And whether they're stock or custom designed, a set of stylin' new rims will put you a step above standard. Chip Foose is justifiably famous partly for his incredible wheel collection, and Foose wheels are now available online and at select shops across the country. (Shoreline Motoring in Huntington Beach, California, put the wheels and tires on my car). Purchasing fancy wheels is, in my opinion, money well spent and makes a tremendous aesthetic difference.

### Pinstriping

Pinstriping is the method of either taping or painting fine lines on a vehicle (or other objects) with a very small paint brush to create either simple lines across the body of the ride to add dimension or intricate designs to add character. Kenneth Howard, nicknamed "Von Dutch," is considered the founder of modern pinstriping. He was a beatnik artist and famous pinstriper of the '50s and '60s. Pinstriping can be done to any vehicle, but it is especially popular within the world of hot rodding. Dennis Ricklefs of DR Designs in L.A. pinstriped the body of my T-Bird with two small beige stripes that match the interior and the beige convertible top. The stripes add dimension and make all the difference.

## Aftermarket Air Boxes/Intake Systems

A good aftermarket intake system can add fifteen to twenty horses to your ride, improve performance, and create a throatier sound. And it's an easy and reasonably priced add-on to install. They are a killer addition to your daily driver that I highly recommend

## Carbon Fiber Body Panels

Carbon fiber hoods or body panels are more popular on import cars. They don't rust, they shave a lot of weight off a vehicle's total poundage, they add horsepower, and they can improve fuel economy. On the right rides, carbon fiber body panels look very cool.

## Roll Cages

Roll cages stiffen the frame, reinforce the roof in case of a rollover and look tough. They're especially practical if you do a lot of off-road driving or own a muscle car. An aftermarket roll cage can add to your ride's looks and make it safer.

## Underbody Diffusers

A rear diffuser, or Venturi, is a panel added underneath the vehicle to rush the air out from under the car as you drive. They come in sheet metal, carbon fiber, or plastic. Diffusers use the Venturi effect to keep turbulence under the car to a minimum, and they help the car grip the road better.

## Air Dams

More and more manufacturers these days are incorporating air dams into standard automotive design, so you might want to ask your dealer if your model is already equipped. An air dam manages the flow of air around the front of a car, pushing it away from the tires and toward the radiator and cooling system. Aftermarket air dams are much more radical than stock air dams, and they usually include integrated bumper and wraparound side panels that extend around the whole front of the vehicle. A lot of tuners have very exaggerated air dams that contribute to their distinctive appearance.

## Powder Coating Vehicle Parts

Powder Coating is a newer technique that involves applying dry paint, or powder, to a car part. The parts are sprayed in a booth with a gun or submerged in powder. Two coats are applied quickly, and the parts are then placed in an oven to bake and cure, forming an outer film that has the same finish as paint. People typically powder coat car frames, suspension systems, brakes, engine parts and wheels to match the color of the vehicle's body or to cut down on maintenance. There is a new powder coating technique done to chrome wheels that eliminates the need to ever have to polish them again. Gotta love that!

I was fortunate enough to experience powder coating firsthand. I powder coated a frame and suspension system during an *Overhaulin'* build at Specialized Powder Coating. It's a cool process that really makes an aesthetic difference. We have a powder coating booth at the *Powerblock* Techcenter as well.

## Hydraulic Lift Kits

Hydraulic lifts, or lifter kits, are added to cars, trucks, or SUVs to gently lift and lower the ride, or any portion of it, with the push of a button. They are used to make a ride look cooler, to raise or lower the vehicle to adjust to various driving conditions, or to raise and lower the truck bed in order to load and unload things more easily. We used them on *Overhaulin'* to trick out cars, and I recently had a monster truck in my *Powerblock* shop that had a Kelderman Air Ride hydraulic lifter bed that lowered and raised the Harley Davidson motorcycle in the back from the bed to the ground with the push of a button.

### Suspension

Your vehicle obviously comes with a stock suspension system, but many people add fancier suspension kits to their rides for a taller or shorter ride height and a different driving feel. Those who do a lot of off-road driving add kits to give the truck more height in order to clear big obstacles and to add more travel room to the springs and shocks for a more cushioned ride. On the other hand, racecar drivers and those wanting a powerful car to sit lower to the ground and have a stiffer, more controlled ride will lower their vehicle's ride height by adding a new

A look from the rear end at the car's differential and the rear axle, springs, and rods that help make the vehicle's suspension system.

suspension system to accomplish this. In both cases, special suspension kits also help improve the vehicle's appearance. I have an Eibach suspension system that lowered my car two inches, giving it a sexier stance and more control when driving.

## *Window Tinting*

Window tinting is the process of applying a film to your vehicle's windows that darkens them to various shades, depending on your preference and within regulations allowed by law where you drive. Windows are tinted both for passenger privacy and also to help lessen the affect of direct sunlight, making the passengers more comfortable during the ride and protecting the vehicle's interior from cracking or fading. There are regulations as to how dark the front side windows and top portion of the windshield can be, because too dark a tint can make it difficult for the driver to see.

## *Supercharger/Blower*

Speed and horsepower junkies are always looking for ways to increase engine power. There are many ways to do this. One way that is safe and inexpensive is by adding a supercharger to the engine. A supercharger forces more air into the combustion chamber, which makes for a bigger explosion, means more fuel can be added to the system, and consequently creates more horsepower. Superchargers increase the intake by compressing the air above normal atmospheric pressure, forcing more air into the engine and creating what's referred to as a "boost." Supercharging adds about 45 percent more horsepower and 31 percent more torque. If I could make hood clearance with a supercharger on my car, I would definitely have added one of these long ago.

Some other modification ideas include tricked out audio systems and fancy speaker boxes, DVD players and LCD screens, safety racing harnesses, special bike and surfboard racks, and cool graphics packages.

These are just some of the ideas for transforming your ride from stock to custom. I believe there is no such thing as a bad modification idea, as long as you're being true to your individualism and are staying safe. Make sure that anything you're doing to your ride doesn't void your warranty. Good luck, have fun with the process, and enjoy your personalized ride!

Now, if you want to go a step further and learn how to install a new crate motor, fabricate a suspension system, or execute any of the more technical ideas for making your ride custom and killer, you should consult specialty manuals, find an expert to do the work, or tune into instructional automotive shows to help teach you. Each weekend I host the automotive *Powerblock* on Spike TV where we show you how to add horsepower to engines and customize cars and trucks. *Powerblock* is comprised of four instructional and entertaining half-hour automotive shows: *Horsepower TV, MuscleCar, Xtreme 4x4,* and *Trucks!* Tune in if you want to learn how to soup up your engines and fabricate your rides. (I couldn't resist a little plug for my favorite automotive how-to shows that have taught me so much!)

Thank you for taking the time to read my book. It was so much fun to share this information with you. I hope you're feeling confident and fired up for a long, exciting road ahead with your ride!

# *Appendix*

On the following pages you'll find all the different maintenance logs I suggested you print and use. They will help keep you organized, while increasing the life of your ride!

# Gasoline Log

| Date | Odometer Reading | Miles Traveled | Gallons Purchased | Miles per Gallon | Fuel Additives |
|------|------------------|----------------|-------------------|------------------|----------------|
|      |                  |                |                   |                  |                |
|      |                  |                |                   |                  |                |
|      |                  |                |                   |                  |                |
|      |                  |                |                   |                  |                |
|      |                  |                |                   |                  |                |
|      |                  |                |                   |                  |                |
|      |                  |                |                   |                  |                |
|      |                  |                |                   |                  |                |
|      |                  |                |                   |                  |                |
|      |                  |                |                   |                  |                |
|      |                  |                |                   |                  |                |
|      |                  |                |                   |                  |                |
|      |                  |                |                   |                  |                |
|      |                  |                |                   |                  |                |
|      |                  |                |                   |                  |                |
|      |                  |                |                   |                  |                |
|      |                  |                |                   |                  |                |
|      |                  |                |                   |                  |                |
|      |                  |                |                   |                  |                |
|      |                  |                |                   |                  |                |
|      |                  |                |                   |                  |                |
|      |                  |                |                   |                  |                |
|      |                  |                |                   |                  |                |

# Maintenance Log (Routine Maintenance)

| Date/Mileage | Location | Service Performed | Parts Replaced | Observations and Warranty Information |
|---|---|---|---|---|
| | | | | |
| | | | | |
| | | | | |
| | | | | |
| | | | | |
| | | | | |
| | | | | |
| | | | | |
| | | | | |
| | | | | |
| | | | | |
| | | | | |
| | | | | |
| | | | | |
| | | | | |
| | | | | |
| | | | | |
| | | | | |
| | | | | |
| | | | | |
| | | | | |
| | | | | |

# Maintenance Log (Repairs and After-Market Add-ons)

| Date/Mileage | Location | Service Performed | Parts Replaced | Observations and Warranty Information |
|---|---|---|---|---|
| | | | | |
| | | | | |
| | | | | |
| | | | | |
| | | | | |
| | | | | |
| | | | | |
| | | | | |
| | | | | |
| | | | | |
| | | | | |
| | | | | |
| | | | | |
| | | | | |
| | | | | |
| | | | | |
| | | | | |
| | | | | |
| | | | | |
| | | | | |
| | | | | |
| | | | | |

## *Credits and Acknowledgements*

Thank you: God, Mom and Dad, Marty Greenberg, Ron Pitkin, Mike Middleton, Denise Little, Mary Sanford, Darren Mann, Donn Golden, Ben Gleib, Chip Foose, Mitch Lanzini, Camee Edelbrock, Frans Hansen, Jordyn Hansen LeValley, John Hamilton, The Edelbrock Corporation, Jon Schultz, Rigoberto Huego, David Hynes, Rob Emerick, and Geoff Ulrich of Victory Management, 3M Corporation, John Torok and Matco Tools, Mario Andretti, Paul Newman, Joe and Patty St. Lawrence, Tom Spychalski, Diane Davis, John Kurtz, Tom duPont, Stacey David, Tony Schumacher, Jesse Combs, Lou Santiago, Marcus J. Fox, Darrin Webb, Dallas Barber, Kristina Duff, Wendell Winfrey and Del Rey Auto, Ivan Alvarez, Liza Anderson, Stacey Pokluda, Chris Kim, George Barris, Jason Christopher, Jake Jundef, James Weir, Kevin Byrd, Neely Shearer, Daniel Zielinski, Kevin Tetz, *The Tyra Banks Show, Extra News.*

Photography and cover image by Jason Christopher
www.jasonchristopher.com

Make-Up by Kristina Duff (www.KristinaDuff.com)

Wardrobe Provided by: B. C. Ethic, Ed Hardy

Diagrams by Dale Glasgow of Glasgow Media
dale@glasgowmedia.com

Additional photography by Greg Meyer

With special thanks to Greg and Mike Meyer of Auto Masters of Green Bay for their help with this project.

## *About the Author*

Courtney Hansen can be seen every Saturday and Sunday on Spike TV's *Powerblock.* This automotive television block features high-performance muscle cars, wild jet drag trucks, industry savvy news, and retrospectives on historic classics. Courtney also stars on Fox Sports Net's (FSN) travel adventure series *Destination Wild,* where she takes viewers on exciting vacation destinations across the United States. She is also the former host of TLC's car makeover show *Overhaulin',* and she hosted *Million Dollar Motors* and *Rides: Biggest Spenders,* also on TLC. Courtney writes a bi-weekly syndicated newspaper column called *Courtney Hansen: Full Throttle,* where she discusses automotive related topics, and a column for *Makes & Models* magazine. She is a celebrity spokesperson for 3M's performance car care products and Matco Tools. Courtney has graced numerous magazine covers and was named one of *FHM*'s "100 Sexiest Women in the World."